A PRO-LIFE MANIFESTO

A
PRO-LIFE
MANIFESTO

Thomas G. Klasen

CROSSWAY BOOKS • WESTCHESTER, ILLINOIS
A DIVISION OF GOOD NEWS PUBLISHERS

First printing, 1988

Printed in the United States of America

Library of Congress Catalog Card Number 87-71890

ISBN 0-89107-469-4

The National Memorial

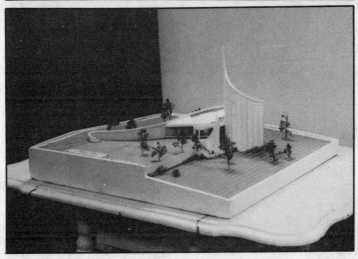

Table of Contents

Introduction

Nothing happening in the world at this moment is more important than the conflict over abortion, except the salvation of souls through Jesus Christ. Abortion robs souls. We in the pro-life movement want to do all we can to end abortion. The question we face is, what will actually stop it?

At the outset, let me draw your attention to two terms. The first is the word "manifesto." A manifesto is a statement of policy or direction. It indicates what needs to be done to bring about a desired end. *A Pro-life Manifesto* is the result of much prayer and guidance of the Holy Spirit. If we on the pro-life side want to win this war, and I believe we do, we will need to pay very careful attention to the principles outlined in this manifesto. We are currently on the wrong track, and if we continue things will only get worse for our cause. The second term is "inner explosion." That is what the pro-life cause must come to realize is our best and surest hope to ending abortion. Inner explosion is what this book is about. Inner explosion is the concept that we have failed to grasp in the effort thus far, and yet it is the most obvious and effective weapon available to us.

As you read *A Pro-Life Manifesto,* please do so with an open mind. It contains many new concepts and a new basic direction that the pro-life forces need to understand. If there is not an immediate and drastic change in policy, I am afraid that the pro-life battle will soon be all over. Certainly it will go on at more personal levels, but as a national campaign to end abortion, we are on the ropes.

Part of the reason for this is a real lack of leadership. We have not been led toward an attainable and well-defined goal. We have wandered listlessly. Much local leadership is burned out and feels frustrated that little has been accomplished. The fault lies with no one individual in particular. It is simply that we are up against something that no one in the movement has had the experience of dealing with before.

Two key sources have given shape and direction to this. The first is the Bible. There is no greater source of wisdom available to us. If we learn from its principles, we can see clearly how to win. The second is history. I believe history holds the key to beating the pro-abortionists, and it is on the basis of what has worked in history that this book is also written.

Study what I have to say closely before you judge. We can win the war, but not without hard and very diligent effort, and a willingness to let go of old concepts and grasp and employ new ones. That is crucial!

God bless you and be with you as you join this struggle for life.

For His Little Ones,
Thomas Klasen

ONE

The
Dilemma

Today, there is a virtual war going on. It is not just a cold war, for there are casualties, tremendous casualties, more than any hot war that has preceded this one. The actual physical casualties are just the tip of the mass of those being victimized in this war. There is a long and growing list of others whose lives have been drastically changed, and in many cases ruined by what is happening. Thus, it is not unlike any other war, for in every conflict there are numerous casualties. But the scars borne by those wounded in this war are visible only by observation of their actions.

The combatants are two very large and powerfully locked forces: the pro-abortionists, who like to be called pro-choice, and the pro-life forces, of which I am a member. At present, the issue centers on the law. One side desires the freedom to end pregnancy, despite the fact that this results in the taking of innocent human life. The other side is attempting to obtain passage of laws which will protect all human life, irrespective of age. That is a very simplistic assessment of what the conflict is about, but to describe the undercurrents, side issues, and varied fronts would be near to impossible. There are multitudes of issues involved here. Each victory scored by a side carries far greater ramifications than most realize. The combat is extremely complicated.

The basic problem is that we do not have laws established that we must obey. What I mean is that there is no law that states that a woman must have an abortion. Nor is there a law that states that she must *not* have an abortion. Whatever a woman believes, she is free to follow. That allows her a choice, but the problem is that in giving her absolute freedom to choose, several other important individuals are denied the right to exercise their choice. Her baby will die not because it has chosen to, but because its mother has decided for it. The father of the child has no choice. He may love his child and desire to let it go on living, but he is denied any legal influence in the decision. He must accept the consequences of a decision in which he is treated as a casual observer.

Strangely enough, society has not been given a choice either. A Supreme Court decision is not necessarily the consent of the governed. It may in fact be in direct opposition to that consent. Yet, because of the nature of the division of powers in the United States, the Court's decision will stand as if Congress had passed a law. The issue is further complicated by the fact that the media have decided that they will not treat abortion according to strict canons of unbiased journalistic professionalism. They have clearly been partial. All too often they have chosen to purposely distort or ignore facts.

The dilemma occurs for the pro-life forces in the realization that we simply cannot legislate a solution. We cannot pass a law that will end abortion in America. The pro-abortionists have been saying that right along, but we in the pro-life camp have not taken their statement very seriously. It is a true statement, and we must begin to assess it as a serious obstacle to overcome. If anti-abortion legislation could be reenacted, it would most assuredly prevent a great number of abortions every year. But the effects of such legislation on the pro-life cause is also a great concern that is not honestly being assessed by the pro-life camp. When analyzed, the pro-life camp seems to be in a no win position, and to a degree we are. Our dilemma is more a matter of our own doing than anything else. There is a solution, but it is not in the way we are going about it at this time. I am not saying we don't need anti-abortion legislation. We desperately need some and we need it soon. We need a law that recognizes *every* human life as unique and desirable, a law that insures that no one—not mother, father, doctor, social worker, society, or anyone else—has the right to destroy innocent life. That is paramount for order and decency in our land.

What I am saying is that we cannot force a woman to accept a legal solution. It simply won't work. If we make abortion illegal, without doing much more than that, it won't solve anything. We will not be addressing the reasons that abortion was a desirable option in the first place. We will see, as we did before the January 22, 1973, Supreme Court decision, a tremendous number of illegal abortions. All abortions are illegal. Just because they are presently sanctioned by human courts doesn't make them legal. Abortion is a direct violation of the laws of God. Consequently, the state has never had, nor will it ever have, the right to pass legislation allowing abortion. Nor does the court have the right to ban states from passing such legislation. We are living in an age of illegal government, an age in which the state has violated the very purpose for which it exists. Until abortion in the United States is banned, and all life receives equal protection by law, we are living in a society governed by a government that has forfeited its right to govern. If you doubt my words, read the Declaration of Independence and even better than that, listen to the Savior when he said, "Render unto Caesar the things that are Caesar's, and unto God the things that are God's" (Mark 12:17).

From those statements it should be clear that I do favor legislation that will protect all human life. Until we have such legislation, we are living in a society that is and will remain in chaos. However, we must not lose sight of the fact that we cannot legislate morality. We cannot pass a law that will force someone to do something, nor can we pass a law that will prevent them from a specific action. Clearly, it is easier to pass a law that forces individuals to perform certain actions. We can do this by establishing agencies to enforce the law. Our nation is full of enforcement agencies. Our judicial system is an enforcement agency. The whole concept of requiring a license for certain functions in society is built on that premise. However, no matter how clearly the law is set down, and how extensive the enforcement, numerous individuals will slip through the cracks. It takes a specific observation of a violation in order to make the law workable. There is a sixty-five mile per hour speed limit law. In order to realize how flagrantly it is violated just drive sixty-five once and you will seem to be standing still in comparison to most of the other traffic. A great many violators are caught, but most are not.

Any attempt to legislate the solution to abortion will fail for exactly the same reason. We will apprehend some offenders, but most we will not. We will, by the passage of a law, discourage some from violating that law, but a great many will simply find a way around it. Illegal drug trafficking provides a good example. We have strict laws banning illegal drug use and dissemination. Yet these laws have done little to curb illegal drug trafficking. The drug problem continues to reach epidemic proportions. This is because no law can stop an undesirable action from taking place if there are individuals who are convinced that what the law is attempting to prevent is desirable for them.

If we are to end abortion in America we must approach it from a completely different angle. We must do much more than pass a law. We must change the attitude of an entire nation. To change attitudes is not easy, but for the vast majority it can be done. Our perspective must change, and in order to change the perspective of this nation we will have to change our strategy. The external pressure we are attempting to exert on the pro-abortionists is not ending abortion, nor is it weakening the other side. The startling truth is it is making the other side stronger. Our own efforts are making matters worse! The honest truth is that we are bringing about our own demise. Unless we acknowledge it soon, we will most certainly lose the fight to end abortion.

There was a point in Jesus' ministry when He was accused of being in league with Satan. He was charged with casting out demons in the name of Satan and by his authority. Jesus' answer was plain and simple: "Any kingdom divided against itself is laid waste; and any city or house divided against itself shall not stand" (Matthew 12:25). What He declared was so obvious, and yet, seldom do we see that principle applied as a means to achieve an end. Nevertheless, there is no power existing more destructive to any organization, even if that is an entire nation, than internal dissension.

External pressure usually knits people together. Adversity is a great unifier. Ties are formed that result in greater resistance to further pressure. External pressure rarely defeats a movement. The clearest and finest example of this is the Christian Church. When the Roman Empire attempted to eradicate Christianity, it did so by persecution. This persecution escalated until it became a policy of extermination. The result was that the church grew at a rate far exceeding what seemed possible. The Romans, by their direct action, were fueling the fire! They were helping to insure that Christianity would be alive and well. As Tertullian, a third-century theologian, said, "The blood of the martyrs is the seed of the Church."

Some people can be intimidated. They run for cover when persecution arises. That is to be expected. There are always weak persons in any group. The overall effect of persecution, however, is that the cause being attacked becomes stronger. Pressure weeds out the weak who were probably a detriment to their cause anyway. Pressure solidifies. In Romans 5:3-4 the Apostle Paul says, "Suffering produces endurance, and endurance character, and character hope." James says it in a bit different way when he states: "Count it all joy, my brethren, when you meet various trials, for you know that the testing of your faith produces steadfastness" (James 1:2-4).

Someone will say, "But that applies to the Christian! It isn't valid for other situations!" We must realize that God-given principles are as valid for the non-Christian as for the

Christian. When trials are encountered endurance is produced. When affliction is met and the reaction is registered, it is almost assuredly one of strength, not weakness. There is an inner purifying that results in greater strength than ever before. External pressure helps build internal strength.

This is mainly a strong spiritual principle, although it has some validity physically. We must not confuse the two. It is the confusion of them that has led one side to viciously attack the other much like a boxer would attack his opponent with repeated blows. The feeling is that a steady barrage of blows will finally knock the opponent to the canvas. Likewise, the pro-life strategy is often a strategy that is an assault upon the opposition by applying strong external pressure in a combative way. Verbal blow after verbal blow is heaped upon the opposition with the intent of destroying their position. Words turn into more and more drastic measures and these eventually lead to even more aggressive measures. Millions of dollars are being spent to keep the combatants strong and ready. Millions of dollars and long hours of effort are spent to keep up a strong and steady barrage.

The effect has been predictably nil. A few abortion clinics have been closed, and we are no closer to ending abortion in America than we were when the tragedy broke upon us. Oh, we are more organized and we have much better weapons, but the abortionists have gotten stronger and more determined as well. The National Organization for Women (NOW) has elected a more determined and aggressive president and strengthened its stand on abortion. It and the other pro-abortion forces have become more and more militant rather than more conciliatory. Recent actions are resulting in more serious confrontations. We have become locked into a hopeless conflict, which does nothing to prevent the deaths of over four thousand babies every day.

We have been fighting this war improperly. We have tried to conquer a spiritual or moral problem through physical means. The results have been too many defeats, or at best, standoffs. We are facing as many losses as victories.

With so many babies dying each day, we cannot afford a standoff!

Let me state quite clearly and without hesitation: I love the people in the pro-life movement, but I don't agree with their methods. At times I cringe at some of the things that are done, but I know what the motivating interest is—to stop the killing. Those in the pro-life movement grieve over the tragedy that is sweeping into more and more homes every day. They feel their guts ache when they view an abortuary or see the twisted and mutilated remains of what was a human baby. They are frustrated over the lack of public support. They are distraught by the vast apathy they see in society. They weep over the growing number of babies that will never share the joy of being held by their mother or father. They get angry over the arrogance and greed of the abortionists. They want only that all life be honored and respected. They, for the most part, don't want revenge or retribution. They just want the killing to end. They want sanity to return to our land. But good intentions don't necessarily make for good strategy. Right now, the pro-life camp is using the wrong strategy.

Those in the pro-life movement must see that, according to our society, they are the aggressors. They blame the press, public indifference, liberals and a host of others. They are failing to see, and it is critical that they do, that it is their own strategy that is causing the problem. They have a cause for which they can hardly miss, and yet, they are missing their goal. They are being viewed as an external force attempting to exert its way upon our society. That is not to judge whether or not they are correct in what they desire to achieve. The fact is that they are not the legal or accepted position in this land. They are right, and if they were listened to the United States would be far better off, but they are perceived as the aggressor, and they are using the tactics of an aggressor. Failure to appreciate that fact will certainly lead to failure in the effort to achieve their goal.

The dilemma is that of an innocent man attempting to

prove his innocence when no one will listen and many even think him guilty. That is exactly the situation the pro-life movement finds itself in. It cannot get people to listen to the evidence. Society is not weighing the evidence—it is reacting to strategy. We cannot change the current situation until we get people to pay attention and to seek the truth. We can get their attention by radical tactics, but we will get few to listen to what we have to say. Nor must we fool ourselves into thinking it is possible to get it through the election process. It will take a complete and drastic change of strategy.

Currently the pro-life cause has patiently presented the facts only to find that the press doesn't want to print them, television doesn't want to show them, and the public doesn't want to hear them. Hope turns to frustration. The thought is that if they won't listen to normal requests, then we have to do something more sensational to get their attention. The spiral continues until those whom the message is aimed at turn away, get angry, or counterreact. The spiral continues until the actions to get attention become more engaging than what the message is. Thus, when certain actions are taken the press is there, not to present the facts of what abortion is doing, but because something sensational is happening. The reaction is horror or anger toward the actions being taken, and not toward the horrible event that is taking place in our midst that has brought about this type of reaction. It feels good to get on the evening news, but it doesn't accomplish much. If anything, the pro-life cause is seen as an extremist movement.

If we are going to attempt to close abortion clinics and end abortion by the current strategy, then the only logical thing to do is to take that strategy to its ultimate conclusion, to take it all the way. We would take the Declaration of Independence at its word and, since we have attempted to change the laws to no effect, we would change the government. That means revolution. Revolution means that we would have to engage in all-out conflict. It would mean serious armed aggression against both the clinics and hospitals that perform abortions and the abortionists themselves.

It would mean that there would be total commitment to-ward eradicating every vestige of abortion in America. Pre-dictably, the government would get involved, and that would mean civil war. There would be little hope of victory for the pro-life cause, and it would be virtually eliminated. There would only be left the embittered loyalists to a dead cause.

Yet, full, armed aggression would be better than to carry out the current method of attempting to end abortion by exerting some aggression, but always not enough to really accomplish anything. That means that a clinic is bombed here or there and some picketing goes on, but little more. The irony is that babies are being ripped apart and the pro-life camp is priding itself in being nonviolent! This is a war. Whoever heard of fighting a war without disturbing or injur-ing anyone?

Armed aggression is a very tempting route to take. Open and tangible results would be seen, and even if it meant defeat—and it would—at least we could go down with our guns blazing. The cause for which we would be sacrificing ourselves would be lost, but at least we would get attention. Abortion would still go on, and there would be stringent and severe punishment for those who attempted to advocate the pro-life position. There would be martyrs on both sides and little would be accomplished beyond that.

If armed aggression were the answer, it would have to be aggression that did not hesitate. It would have to be done on a large scale, and more than a few abortion clinics would have to be destroyed. To succeed, it would require the destruction of all hospitals or clinics that performed abor-tions. Heroes who would lay down their life for the cause would have to come forth. Armies would need to be orga-nized. Companies producing abortifacients would have to be bombed and their employees terrorized. In short, we would have to be willing to plunge ourselves into civil war.

While at times it seems that we are headed for just such a scenario, the conditions are not right for that to happen. The pro-life forces don't have the aggressive, radical leadership necessary to accomplish that goal. There is not enough cohesion in the pro-life camp. We don't have the masses of people who are so enraged that they would sacrifice all to further this cause. No, the pro-life leadership is bound to work within the system. It will not take up this cause, even though it is much more urgent than the cause that started the Civil War, because the zeal is not there that was present then. The reason is not clear. Perhaps we need to find a way to make the pro-life cause affect everyone's pocketbook as the cause of the Revolution did. Perhaps we need to develop a strong personable champion that will share a vision of a world without death houses.

In many ways, our cause is a strange one. We are fighting against something that is killing more lives than we can even comprehend, but what it is not doing is probably more important than what it is doing: it is not hitting people where they hurt—in their bankbooks. It is not interfering with most religious beliefs, although it should be a festering sore in people's conscience. It does not invade privacy. It happens around us daily, and few notice or care because it doesn't upset anyone. There are no freight cars being loaded with victims. There are no screaming women being dragged into abortion clinics. The individuals that attract attention are labeled as fanatics and soon dismissed. At this time, there is nothing taking place that is getting anyone excited, and that includes most of those in the pro-life camp.

We are beginning to see the pro-life movement face the situation where it is becoming more and more difficult to get anyone excited about its cause. It has tried desperately for years to change conditions in America, and it has failed. The pro-abortionists have been hoping that discouragement will set in and the whole movement will silently fade away. They have been predicting that very thing, and their predictions are coming true. They have said that a few diehards will remain, but the broad base of public support will gradually fall. Horrifyingly, that is what is beginning to happen. If the trend continues, abortion will be an accepted fact in America, and it will be an accepted fact about which very little will be able to be done. If there is a danger facing the pro-life cause today it is the danger of apathy and eventual despair, a danger for which the pro-life movement has only itself to blame. It has no strong unified plan of action. It has no visualized goal around which to rally people. It is currently wandering aimlessly in hope of a miracle.

If you doubt that this is happening, try appealing to the general public on this issue. You will find very little sympathetic response. It has nothing to do with the rightness or wrongness of the issue. It has everything to do with whether or not the cause affects the people to whom you are talking. The vast majority of Americans are simply not affected. Thus, while they shudder that babies are being torn apart, they simply dismiss it by denying the babies' humanity, by calling abortion a "tragedy" but still necessary, or by coming up with a myriad of other excuses. This catalogue of denial allows them to be cushioned from the reality they won't recognize. They are not able to see the correlation between the abortion issue and their life. Raise their taxes, and they see all kinds of issues to become excited about. Kill a child in the womb and they yawn. Announce a killer loose in the city and doors are locked and newscasts monitored. Murder a baby, and no one notices; life simply goes on.

Why? It doesn't affect them directly. This is being done by a woman who has a difficult decision. They accept the argument that she has a right to do to her own body as she pleases, because it lets them off the hook. The responsibility is hers. The death sentence is carried out without reporters. A problem is simply eliminated, silently and unfeelingly. After all, what is legal is moral. At least that's how many Americans see it. Abortion is a necessary evil—unfortunate, but necessary. And after all, they reason, it does more good than harm. As shocking as those opinions may seem, that is how things are being viewed. The truth is that people simply don't care.

One other aspect of abortion that needs to be discussed is the attempt to show the public exactly what abortion is and what it is doing. This attempt is failing, and to understand why we must understand the logic of what is happening. The phenomenon is called denial. For one to really appreciate the way denial works we must turn to Nazi Germany. It is difficult to imagine that the German people could have tolerated what was happening in their midst. Yet, over six million Jews were led to their death as their countrymen stood by and watched. How could a whole nation not react when strong and drastic action was called for? How is it that the church, an institution that should have screamed foul, stood by and allowed this to happen? When we begin to grasp the answer to questions like these, we will start to understand the situation in the United States today.

The reason six million Jews were killed in Germany and nearly twenty million babies have been killed in America is because of denial. Denial comes into play when we know something is wrong, but the action required to stop it demands a greater self-sacrifice than we are willing to make. Hitler had brought prosperity back to Germany. He brought jobs, dignity and hope. The people realized that under Hitler there were some deeply disturbing things happening. World War I had left the German people void of personal and national dignity. Ever so quickly Hitler was restoring that. With jobs, dignity, and prosperity he had also brought a very well-organized political machine. He was taking control of people's lives, but he was giving them something in return. To resist Hitler was to resist the hope and future of Germany—at least so they reasoned. People were being helped. Most people were seeing their lives made better, and those who weren't believed that Hitler was going to do something for them soon.

The horrifying element is that Hitler was able to aim his persecution at a specific group of people and get away with it. His target was the Jews, much because of anti-Semitism and more because they were a prime, easy-to-identify target. That is what made the Holocaust work. The group being persecuted was identifiable. It could have been any number of identifiable groups, but it was at the Jew that Hitler pointed his deadly finger. The Jews were separated from the rest of society, and so long as people did not protest too loudly, they were safe from being included with them. It seems incredible, but the people who turned them in were often their neighbors, friends, and associates—people who had associated with them for years.

Certainly there were those who stood against what Hitler was doing, but they were in a minority. Those who protested too loudly found themselves in the camps with the Jews. That fact is well known. Most chose not to protest, but to watch silently as the Jews were being led away to die. There were many who died in protest, or attempted to resist or protect the lives of those who were sentenced to die. Sadly, there were far too few heroes in Germany, far fewer than were needed to make Hitler see that his policy was causing severe dissension within his ranks. Later, when the killings were over and the truth exposed, those who sat stunned over what had happened could only deny they knew. Without question they did know. They didn't act because they were afraid—afraid for their lives and afraid to lose the economic gains they had enjoyed.

Were they cowards? Yes, but it is the same cowardice that abides in all peoples of all nations. Even the Jews who died had that same indwelling cowardice. It is part of fallen man, and has nothing to do with a particular people or race. Hitler simply exploited that fact, and we still shudder over the result. It has displayed itself numerous times in history and in peoples of various backgrounds, and it has happened all too often since. The German people were sad victims. Yet, each of us, without exception, has been its victim in similar situations and circumstances. It is a plain, simple truth. We have this built within ourselves, and it is part of that inherited nature called sin. We cannot escape from it, while we remain in the flesh, but we can learn and understand what makes it tick.

Adolf Hitler, being under the influence of Satan, knew how to use this nature far too craftily. The German people succumbed not because they were a nation of cowards, but because Hitler used what is common to human nature and turned it against the German people. Hitler was insanely

25

mad. Yet, to be mad doesn't mean that one cannot be exceedingly crafty. Hitler was a brilliant fool, for he could have been a great leader and hero, but he allowed his blind demonic leadings to plunge himself and the nation he led into shame.

This is not meant to be a book on Hitler and Germany, but there are some important truths to be gleaned from Nazi Germany that can be used to understand the pro-life dilemma. First, a specific group of people were singled out for persecution. Second, unless people became directly involved, they were fairly safe. Third, there was a perceived economic benefit arising from the actions taken. Fourth, there was a cause around which to rally. Fifth, the victims were silenced and removed from the mainstream of society. Sixth, it arose under the proper economic, social, and political conditions.

Every one of these factors is found in the abortion controversy of today. In the next chapter I am going to discuss each of these factors and how they relate to the pro-life movement. To understand the strategy that I am going to propose to end abortion, the factors that make its existence possible must first be understood. By ending abortion I mean much more than making it illegal. I mean that we have the power to make abortion odious to everyone. We have the power to lay it bare for what it is and to effectively destroy it and to gain as allies groups now supporting it.

In reference to what I have said in this chapter, let me close with the following quote from Scripture:

> Rescue those who are unjustly sentenced to death; don't stand back and let them die. Don't try to disclaim responsibility by saying you didn't know about it. For God, who knows all hearts, knows yours, and He knows you knew! And He will reward everyone according to his deeds (Proverbs 24:11-12).

TWO

Why
Abortion
Thrives

Abortion is thriving in America. That may seem like an odd statement coming from a pro-lifer, but when one looks at the evidence, that is the unavoidable conclusion. Consider for a moment what is happening. A woman, who is with child, is being persuaded that the best decision she can make is to take that child and kill it. Not only is she to take the child and have it destroyed, but she is going to have to pay for the murder. Also, she is to be glad or relieved that her ordeal is over, and she is expected not to have, or at least to admit to, any physical or psychological consequences.

In order for all of this to be possible there has had to have been a massive silence on the part of the media. Women's organizations have had to get on the bandwagon, backing a concept that threatens their basic goals as if it were a great liberator rather than a great enslaver. The government has had to support abortion, as it has. The church has had to sit quietly by and let it all happen as if this were an issue that does not concern it. Those who are fighting for the unborn have to be more concerned about sustaining their individual organizations than achieving unity and strength within the movement. The general public has to remain apathetic about this issue, and therefore remain unmovable. All these things have taken place, and more. We have virtually established what seems impossible. We have accepted, no, we have *hailed,* abortion as a great liberator of women. Women now have a choice. They can bear children or they can abort them. If their primary system of contraception fails, if they have one, they can correct the situation by having an abortion.

How can this be? How can we allow the carnage that is taking place in America to continue? Why does abortion continue to thrive? Why is it that with all the medical, psychological, and spiritual evidence available we cannot see clearly to condemn this savage practice and return to civility? How is it possible that in a nation dedicated to the rights and liberty of all of its citizens such a diametrically opposite standard has arisen and survived? To understand the answer we must look at the factors that I mentioned at the end of Chapter 1 and were the very factors that ushered in and sustained the Nazi Holocaust. It is in understanding these that we can begin to formulate a strategy that will end abortion and return our land to sanity.

The first thing we need to understand about abortion is that a specific class of people have been singled out for persecution. It is no secret that abortion threatens only a very specific group of individuals. The child in the womb has been identified as and has become an ideal victim. An ideal victim is one that is incapable of offering resistance. It is common knowledge that the most vulnerable of society require the greatest protection. God designed the womb as a safe haven for the small child to grow and develop. The womb is a very secure setting for life to begin. The child is enfolded by its mother's body. Development takes place at a very fast rate with the most obvious form of communication an occasional kick. Almost everyone else, except the mother, doesn't even know the child is present. She becomes aware of the presence of this new life very early. She is the one who ultimately decides if that child becomes a precious life to protect or a victim to destroy. The victim is oblivious to her decision. The child is serenely growing within its safe haven, unaware that its life may be in imminent danger.

When the child is designated to be killed, it becomes a

victim of the abortionist. At this point something very critical takes place, namely, silence. The last thing both the abortionist and the mother want is a kicking, screaming, surviving victim. Occasionally one of the victims survives long enough to make a torturous impact upon all the conspirators. The screaming cry of this "blob of flesh," this "product of conception," shatters everyone's nerves. Swift actions must be taken to quickly suppress the truth. The child, alone and defenseless, is either left to die, strangled, or denied lifesaving support. Each cry must seem like an eternal cry to all present, each scream an eternal infliction agonizing to the very soul. This living victim has been the nightmare of many. The baby isn't supposed to be a baby. The baby isn't supposed to live.

Abortionists want young victims. The earlier the age, the less chance of a living survivor. The younger the victim, the less chance that there will be pieces of visible evidence that this was a baby and not a blob of flesh. Many women have gone to pieces when the "product of their pregnancy" was visualized and they saw nothing resembling a mass of tissue. They saw a small, but very recognizable human being. For some it was merely a piece of that human, but clearly identifiable nonetheless. At that point their error becomes horribly, but irreversibly, known.

The abortionist will also kill older children. It is much more complicated and much more costly. There are greater risks and a much greater chance of embarrassing consequences. The law offers virtually no protection even up to a few moments before normal delivery. When there is a dollar to be made, and for this filthy job there is, someone will be there to make it. The killer may be considered a respected member of society, but God is a better judge of that. Money reduces morals.

Mother Theresa called abortion a nation's greatest poverty. It is a poverty of morals, love, compassion, and decency. In Nazi Germany the Jews were herded into boxcars and taken away from public view. They were taken to places where the foul deeds would be done in private. The rest of

31

society had an idea what was happening, but since it wasn't going on right in their midst, they denied it. Out of sight, out of mind. If you weren't a Jew, and you didn't cause problems, you were safe from the same fate.

Children in the womb face a different yet related situation. They are hacked to pieces and quickly disposed of. The late-term pregnancies present a more difficult problem, but the incinerators or garbage dumps are readily available. The Jews were incinerated or buried in mass graves. The mass graves weren't much better than a garbage dump. There have been discoveries of masses of aborted babies disposed of in garbage dumps in the United States. While many people are moved by seeing these or hearing about them, most of the population remains stoically unaffected.

There is an interesting psychology at work here. An immediate threat or perceived threat arouses immediate action. A killer such as AIDS initially caused very little public anxiety. That changed decisively when it was discovered that AIDS could affect heterosexuals as well as homosexuals. Until something is perceived as a *personal* threat, most people will remain unconcerned. For people to get concerned about a threat that does not directly affect them, it must be aimed at a pitiable person. That is why the abortionists want to portray the child in the womb as an anonymous blob, not as a helpless, innocent baby. We don't mind if blobs are killed, but people get excited if babies are being killed. Thus, abortionists use dehumanizing language. It does not concern most people if a "product of conception" is terminated, but if a tiny baby in the womb is butchered, many will react negatively.

To understand the little word games that are being used, it is necessary to begin to listen to the language that is being employed. It is not by accident that the terminology is the way it is. It is not accidental that the goal of the abortionist's debate and rhetoric is to focus upon the woman and her plight rather than the baby and its plight. The woman is visible and able to generate sympathy. If the baby is hidden, and its humanity denied, it can be killed and most of society will not even question it. Notice how sympathetic words are used to describe the woman: "her body," "her right to choose," "between her and her doctor," "safe abortion," "a right that is hers and hers alone," "men do not have to bear children," and on and on go the list of descriptions designed to gain our sympathy and approval. A counterstrategy is used in describing the unborn child. When it is terminated it is almost as if a cancerous growth has been removed and not a living baby.

Those who are not directly involved are fairly safe. But if someone does choose to get involved, there can be un-pleasant consequences. On the surface it would seem that this does not apply to the pro-life issue. No one is dragging pro-lifers into abortion clinics and killing them along with the babies. In Nazi Germany it was very dangerous for an individual to attempt to protect the life of a Jewish citizen. The most common result of such efforts was that the de-fender ended up in a concentration camp as well. There were thousands of individuals who lost their life because of their stand in protecton of their fellow citizens. Opposition to Hitler's policies was a dangerous road to take.

Something similar is beginning to happen in America. Increasingly, pro-life activists are being persecuted and har-assed. No one is yet being put to death, but there have been attacks. The pro-life activists are not being butchered, but they are being put through legal hassles far out of proportion to the actions that have led to those suits. In some instances the courts have attempted to proscribe the right of peaceful assembly. In other cases sentencing has been much more severe than similar cases not involving abortion clinics. Women's organizations on the pro-abortion side have de-clared war on the pro-life activists. Today, in the United States, there is a considerable risk by becoming involved.

The pro-life activist is an individual of considerable courage. I know some of the more well-known activists, and they aren't raving maniacs as the press has attempted to make them. They love mother and child. They simply see abortion as cold-blooded murder and they want the killing to end. They are worthy of our support and encouragement. The pro-abortionists will fail to silence the pro-life activists for the same reason the pro-life activists will fail to silence the pro-abortionists. Persecution produces endurance.

It also produces benefits. Few people realize that the Germans benefited greatly from the extermination of six million Jews. The Jews who went to the camps left behind goods, land, businesses, and jobs which were confiscated and used as the authorities saw fit. Some went to the local residents, some to the state, and some into the hands of corrupt officials. I think the picture is clear. There is always someone who will do anything for money.

Abortion too produces benefits. The cost of an abortion varies from state to state, region to region. It also depends upon the circumstances, such as the age of the child. The older the baby, the more costly. Abortion is over a half-billion dollar industry, and that probably is a very conservative figure. Today, more and more abortionists are discovering ways to profit from the aftereffects of abortion, and this has now become a multi-billion dollar industry! Imagine, each year people in the United States alone are paying nearly one billion dollars to have babies executed. It is no wonder that abortionists have so many well-paid lobbyists. It is no wonder that an organization such as Planned Parenthood backs abortion and even runs some clinics. They also receive nearly one hundred million dollars each year of our tax money, thanks to government programs that turn their back on this issue. Most pro-life organizations are attempting to operate on budgets less than a fraction of that amount. Talk about David and Goliath! But remember, David won because God fought for him!

There is an even more disturbing aspect relating to the economics of abortion, namely, the perceived benefit of what is taking place. Hitler accused the Jews of robbing Germany of her wealth and prosperity. Some actually bought this lie. Today, we hear talk about the cost of raising children and the financial hardship these babies would present.

We hear abortion being defended because the child that would be born would cost the taxpayers money. We hear arguments that attempt to justify abortion on the basis of a perceived economic threat to a woman's or family's well-being. The value of the life is never assessed. What is being done is that fears are being fueled so that the issue becomes an economic one rather than a moral issue. It is the same method the old sleight of hand artist uses—focus the attention off what is important and onto a diversion. The result is that the unsuspecting person becomes an easy victim. Satan knows how to fuel both our fears and our greed. In the perceived economic factor he is a master. We have determined that the value of our own comfort far outweighs the value of a human life. That is a very fearful path to start down, but we have started down it, and God help us if we don't realize that it leads to wholesale murder.

We also have a massive suppression of truth. What a terrible path we start down when we decide that a cause is best served by suppressing the truth. We have at work in the pro-abortionist camp a whole host of planned lies, or to be generous, deceptive statements. It is a multifront deception that is attempting to dupe the public, dupe a woman contemplating an abortion, and certainly to dupe their own organizations. What is the most frightening about it is that there has been excessive media cooperation. Without the cooperation of the media, the lies would have been dispelled long ago.

In his book *Aborting America,* Dr. Bernard Nathanson, a former leading abortionist who is now pro-life, describes how he and those involved in attempting to influence public opinion made up statistics that they knew were totally out of line with reality. The media, we are told, swallowed them without ever investigating or questioning their validity. The press hasn't changed much even today. It is prone to accept the pro-life arguments as being contrary to women's rights. They simply fail to do a good job of investigative reporting. There is a tremendous story awaiting a good investigative reporter, if that reporter has the guts to take on the entire liberal establishment, including the newspaper he or she works for.

The press is being fed influential lies and reporting them as fact. There are several national organizations that are determined that the public does not hear both sides of the issue, or at least that the pro-life side is greatly distorted. What is so painful is that the pro-life cause has been playing right into their hands. Instead of picketing abortion clinics, they should be picketing newspaper offices and television studios.

To be able to understand the pro-life dilemma you have to be a pro-life advocate and attempt to get the truth printed or aired. In plain, simple words, the media refuse to do it. One argument I was confronted with is that abortion is "too violent" to show on TV. If they really believed that, it would directly contradict another of their basic premises—that the "product of conception" is merely a "blob of tissue." It is nonsense to talk about violence against a blob of tissue. If abortion is "too violent," it is because it involves the destruction of innocent human life. You can't have it both ways. The truth is that the media have bought into the feminist argument. They have committed themselves to the feminist idea of abortion as a woman's "right." Therefore, they are prone to believe the feminists and their allies and reject the views of their opponents.

There is much to be said about the media and their suppression of the truth. However, lies are being disseminated in two other important places. First, in the woman's movement, groups like NOW and NARAL (National Abortion Rights Action League) have dedicated themselves to the concept that abortion is more important than truth. I say that because it is obvious that these groups know very well that they are advocating the destruction of innocent human life. However, since it is for a good cause, women's rights, it is justified. Were not life and death issues at stake, it would be humorous to observe the juggling act used to maintain their position. Yet the endless rationales for abortion do absolutely nothing to establish the right of one group of people (women and their doctors) to kill off another group of people (unborn babies).

Nevertheless, the lies and half-truths continue on in such slogans as these: "A woman has a right over her own body"; "the child may grow up unwanted"; "women will use coat hangers"; "women will go to pieces psychologically"; "a woman has a right to self-fulfillment in a career"; "there are enough people on welfare already;" "the child won't be loved." On and on the list continues. The strategy is to move the focus away from the real issue and onto side issues. The problem is that these lies are helping to kill one and one-half million babies each year.

While the above practice is a horrible distortion of the truth, there is an even greater lie being told (which will be treated in more depth in a later chapter). It is that lie that is told to a woman who goes to a clinic or referral service. She is told that her pregnancy can be terminated because it is not a child but a blob of flesh or a mass of tissue. She is also told that abortion is a simple, safe, and painless procedure. The clinic will use any form of deception to insure that she not know the truth. Go into a clinic or counseling center and see if there are pictures, accurate pictures, of what the child looks like. If you are a pregnant woman, attempt to have the truth presented to you, and you will discover how far they will carry their lies. Even if you aren't pregnant, go into one of the clinics and tell them you are. Be hesitant about an abortion and then listen as they begin their propaganda campaign against your baby, and also against your future well-being. It is eye-opening. How do I know? I've talked to numbers of victims of the abortionist lies. These guilt-ridden women wish only one thing—that they had been told the truth so they could have made an honest decision. Is that asking too much? Yet, our Supreme Court has even taken that right away from women.

An entire book can and should be written about the lies that are being told to support abortion. We buy into those lies because we need to. If we admit that they are lies, then we must face the horror of what is being done. We are then compelled to act. If we fail to act, we betray our own sense of moral goodness. For many, it is much easier to just accept the lies. Abortion is surviving on lies. The pro-abortion forces know that their lies could never stand the light of truth.

One strategy they have tried is to link abortion to a noble cause—the struggle for women's rights. Ironically, it was this linkage that was fundamental in the defeat of the ERA amendment, since it signaled an alarm which said to the rest of the population that the ERA backers were fanatical in their efforts. If abortion had not been so directly linked to the women's rights movement, it probably would not be legal today, and the ERA, perhaps, would be a reality. Without the intertwining of abortion with women's rights, abortion would be looked upon in a more rational perspective by the hard-core women's rights groups. A cleverly devised myth has arisen that if women lose abortion rights they will have suffered a disastrous defeat. That isn't true, but they have come to believe that lie. The real truth is that abortion exploits women.

This fanaticism almost, and I say almost, makes the repeal of the abortion laws impossible. Opposition to abortion is practically a traitorous act for a woman to commit. Nevertheless, millions of women are reacting against abortion, but it is rare to see them in such radical groups as NOW. There are very strong women's groups, such as Eagle Forum and WEBA, that stand directly opposed to abortion because of what it does to women, babies, and our country.

One of the keys to ending abortion in America is to disenchant the women's movements as to the necessity of maintaining abortion to achieve women's rights. In fact, we must go even further and make it clear that if abortion is maintained as a necessity to achieve rights, then those rights will never be achieved. Abortion must become odious to women's rights even in the more fanatical circles.

Whenever mass persecution occurs, the victims are silenced and removed from the rest of society. In Germany they herded the Jews into boxcars and took them to isolated places. If the German people could have seen what was going on, it would have made an immense difference. They knew, for the most part, what was happening, but to know and to have to watch are two entirely different things. In order for the Nazi persecution of the Jews to work, the Jews had to be removed from society. They became nonentities.

A baby in the womb cannot be shipped off to a camp. But it can be removed from society in a more subtle but equally effective way. The method is to deny the humanness of the unborn child and declare that it is nothing more than a growth. If this lie is dramatically presented and repeated enough times, many people will swallow it. It takes a big lie and effective blocking techniques to accomplish this in to-day's society, but it is being done.

This is really a form of propaganda, very effective prop-aganda, and it is being carried out by prominent persons who hold positions of great respect. Again, to emphasize the point, the media have cooperated fully. Efforts to get the media to present even the known facts have been less than fruitful. The media claim that they do not want to become involved in a political issue, but this is much more than a political issue. We are discussing life and death issues. We are discussing the wholesale destruction of millions of lives. What we are experiencing is another form of removal. If the general public is not told what we are dealing with, they are removed from its consequences. Thus, the lie can be propa-gated because it is not exposed by the media. The media's cooperation is necessary to dupe the public and to keep them isolated from the child. It will take some real courage for the mass media of this country to take on the powerful pro-abortion groups, but if television and newspapers are to engender any respect, they must do it.

The nonentity status ascribed to the child is reinforced by the sterile surgical setting of the clinic or hospital. The fact that a hospital allows abortions seems to give the whole procedure some credibility. After all, would a hospital allow something that is not morally right? The answer is simply, yes, they would. They too follow the rationale that what is legal is moral. Abortion is legal, therefore it can be allowed and must be moral. The child becomes of no concern; only the mother matters. Thus, the child loses its identity by being treated as a growth to be removed. The child does not have to be silenced—its scream is a silent one. Only those that survive the operation ever get a few precious moments to scream. What a tragic end to a young, beautiful life.

It took the proper social, economic and political conditions to bring about abortion. All the above factors are important, but without the proper atmosphere, without other conditions providing a perfect incubator for that growth, abortion probably would not have become the cancerous tumor that it is. The United States was ready for a catastrophe such as abortion.

We were ripe for something of this nature because of the triumph of the liberal social agenda. We were entering into a very permissive society. The Playboy philosophy had taken hold, and various forms of media had taken rather bold steps beyond what they had ever dared, and they survived. There had been a revolt against established values, and we entered the decade of the pill. Rock music, the sexual revolution, easy access to contraception, depravity in the arts, and a whole host of other factors combined to loosen former restrictions. The society that once held so many things in check was simply taken over by a new philosophy centered in the self. Do your own thing became the common point of view. Former bonds were being separated, and abortion was to come along and separate a woman from the necessity of bearing children.

Politically we entered a liberal age. The emphasis was upon new ideas. We were exploring space and burning bras. We were a country on the move and women's rights groups began to see progress. Politicians were attuned to what women were demanding, and the Supreme Court was not oblivious to the political pressure that was being brought to bear. On January 22, 1973, that Court spawned one of the greatest monsters since the *Dred Scott* decision. It classified a whole group of people as nonentities. From now on, the child in the womb was fair game to any manner of savagery available. We had entered an age void of moral compassion. Our nation will forever be stained with the blood of the innocents. We sold out the Republic. We no longer had the right to claim, "With liberty and justice for all."

The hearts of the German people had to have waxed very hard as each day thousands of people were eliminated from their midst, often with their full cooperation. Today, we see thousands of people disappear from our midst, often with full cooperation and even coercion of those around them. Parents push a daughter to the abortuary. A father pushes his wife or girlfriend. A friend pushes her friend. Social workers, Planned Parenthood, and a host of other advocates of abortion pressure women to destroy their babies. There is a fanatical desire to abort babies. It is fanaticism that comes directly from the prince of darkness. It leaves the future of this nation much in doubt.

With this has arisen a very common but sad phenomenon, the all too silent church. There are some churches that are taking official stands, but that is all they are, for there are not strong, official actions as well. The key area, the pulpit, is strangely silent. The church has closed its eyes so that it could be about more important business. In the meantime millions of babies die. Their mothers have destroyed them as the church has sat silently by and allowed it to be. The church was equally as silent in Germany. It lost its credibility, and when the horror had finally ended, it had no excuse. There were a few champions then, but not many. There are a few champions again today, but as then, there are few indeed.

The conditions that existed then run parallel to those that exist today. We have entered into a dramatic new age, and the outcome is in the hands of a few brave individuals who stand between the crushing machinery of the abortionist mentality and the total destruction of moral goodness. It is the prayer of many that just as in Nazi Germany, the whole nightmare will come to a grinding halt and the people will awaken from their hypnotic state to the reality of a world in need of compassion and healing. The archvillain will be dead, and there will be the tragic pieces to knit together into a meaningful whole.

Abortion thrives because we have let it thrive. Abortion thrives because the few brave but outnumbered individuals who stand opposed to it are unsure how to stop it. It can be stopped, but not unless we change the way it is being confronted. We have to inject saline into its system, and that will require a new and radical approach. We have seen why it is alive; now let's begin to devise a strategy that will make it die.

THREE

Frustrated
Attempts

There have been many ways that different groups have tried to end the slaughter of the innocents. None of them has been very successful. The reason for their lack of success is not that they were not honest or sincere attempts to present the truth, but rather that they were based upon a false premise. Take those who desire to change the law through education. It is felt by that group that if we present enough people with the truth there will be a public outcry to end abortion. Logically that would seem to make sense. However, I can point to instance after instance where those who sought out an abortion knew exactly what they were doing. They understood totally that they were taking an innocent life, but they did it because it was legal and it seemed to offer a solution to a nearly unsolvable problem.

I can say without hesitation that the leaders of the pro-abortion camp know every bit as much about life in the womb as the pro-life camp does. They understand that we are dealing with a well-formed baby. That is why they so vehemently cloak their language. They know that if they admit the truth, their position would be weakened, indeed destroyed. Their concern is not about a child; it is centered upon the woman and her rights. The child in the womb is seen as an obstacle to those rights. Every cause has a victim, and the unborn child is the necessary victim of the pro-abortionists' cause. The child in the womb is expendable. If

45

that sounds sick to you, welcome to the club. It is very sick indeed. We can take that one step further and point out that physicians who perform abortions know what they are doing, as do the nurses who attend the doctor. We have available rather frank statements from such individuals, and their admission of a true knowledge of what is happening in an abortion is rather shocking.

Education has not stopped the increase of teenage pregnancy, nor has it reduced the drug problem. Young girls do not get pregnant because they don't know that sex produces babies. Oh, there is an occasional exception, but in the majority of cases they were well aware that they were taking a very big chance. Nor has contraception alleviated the problems. It has lured teenagers into a false sense of security. It has certainly made them more promiscuous. We have opened doors for our children and told them that they can feel free to enjoy the pleasures involved since we have eliminated or greatly reduced the risk. Thousands of young people face a terrible crisis because of that lie. Yet, it is being told again and again across our nation in our schools. Perhaps the organization that is most responsible for the state of affairs that now faces our young people is Planned Parenthood. What is sad, and makes me and many others angry, is that our tax dollars are going to support the garbage that that organization is putting out. It is time that we put an end to this nonsense.

The drug problem in the United States is reaching epidemic proportions. We have been flooded with education on this subject, yet the problem continues to grow. Education has not solved the problem at all. In fact, as government studies are beginning to realize, it increased the problem. Again, when faced with a problem that arises out of a basic human drive, education will not do much to alleviate it.

I don't mean to undervalue education as a tool or weapon against an evil such as abortion. What I am attempting to do is state a somber fact. We must not begin to think that abortion will end as a result of educating the public.

Education campaigns are great for stirring up people, giving the impression that something is being accomplished when it is not, using up much time, money and effort, and generally generating the feeling that we are doing something effective. The truth is, education campaigns do little to reach the people who really need to be reached. Most education campaigns, and this is true of pro-life ones, end up preaching to the already converted.

There is a move for more and more direct action. It is felt that such strategies will do much to attain our goals. I am familiar with some of the better-known pro-life activists, and I have a great deal of respect for their courage and determination. They will stop at nothing to focus community attention on their cause. Attention is a necessary ingredient to solving the problem, for without that attention the general public is hardly aware of the presence of those who protest the slaughter that is going on around us. It keeps the public tense, and that is important. The presence of those who protest the killing of the unborn arouse the public, and they are and will remain a vital element in the fight to end abortion. The clearest evidence of that is that it is at those individuals that the other side has leveled its deadliest weapons. Oddly enough, they are playing right into the activist's hands. The activist has them pushed into a corner. They have found that ignoring them will not make them cease, and attacking them doesn't deter them either.

Curiously enough, the pro-abortionists don't know how to handle those in the activist camp. They seem to be choosing alternatives that are adding fuel to the fire. When the abortionist is acting the most vehemently against the activist, the TV cameras roll even more surely. While the activists may appear to be somewhat fanatical to the general public, they are putting abortion on the screen and in the newspapers. The message is clear—someone is upset about the tragedy that is happening around us. Someone is saying that this isn't a neat surgical procedure taking place, but rather it is cold-blooded murder. Without the activists the public would go even more soundly to sleep than it is already.

While all that may seem to indicate that activism is the key to ending abortion, it isn't. Activists will continue to play a key role and remain a thorn in the abortionist's side, but they will not stop the death peddlers. They may close a few abortion clinics here and there, but they will not end the struggle. It takes real courage to do what they are doing, just as surely as it took courage to do some of the crazy things the women's activists did. They are warm-up acts for the main attraction, and while I would like to believe that activists are the key to ending abortion, I cannot. Activists will remain an important element in the war to end murder in America, but they are not the final answer. Like those who see education as their main function, they are playing a part but are not the back-breaking key.

Another strategy being used to end the fight against abortion is to try to elect people who reflect the pro-life philosophy. Thus, if enough Senators and Representatives are elected, we can simply vote abortion out of existence. National Right to Life, one of the largest pro-life organizations in the United States, has adopted this strategy to end abortion. It has spent millions of dollars attempting to change the balance in Congress in favor of the pro-life cause. While this seems like a plausible strategy, it has some serious deficiencies. If we can change the balance of Congress, and if we can get a constitutional amendment passed, then we will have finally ended legal abortion. But the conflict will continue. One problem is that we have not been able to change the makeup of Congress enough to pass such legislation. While it seems that we have made progress, we are in reality not much closer to changing the law this way than we were in previous years. In fact, we have recently lost precious ground. Can we afford to wait every two years to see if we can do something more significant than we have done? *No!* Every two years costs us three million babies! I know that those who support this method disagree and feel that we are making progress, but they are in reality fooling themselves. We will lose if we continue to pursue this method, and I don't believe that the future of our nation will allow us to lose.

The sad truth is that it will probably take years for pro-life legislation to pass, if ever. When we realize that over one and one half million babies are lost each year, we simply cannot wait years. To be very blunt, we are dumping our funds and resources down the drain on a cause that will not work. That is not to say that we shouldn't be voting for pro-life candidates; we should. However, it is a well-known fact that the pro-life cause has been used by politicians to help them get votes, but they have worked very little for the pro-life cause once they have reached office. If they believe that abortion is murder of innocent babies, and that is what it means to be pro-life, then shouldn't this be the most important issue that faces them? Anyone, whether it be an organization or an individual, who believes that Congress is going to end abortion is sadly mistaken.

Currently we have a President who favors the pro-life cause. With such a man leading our government we would expect that there would be great pressure to change the law. I have seen little evidence of that pressure. We are in truth getting lip service. Politicians have one thing in common— they make promises which they rarely deliver in concrete action. I am afraid that this issue, as vital as it is, is little different. Congress can be gotten to act, but the strategy for doing that has to be much different than what it is now. We will not get them to act just because we have a group of voters that wants it a certain way. We would need something more than a coalition. There are thousands of coalitions now petitioning Congress for everything under the sun. The pro-life cause is but one, and an underfinanced one at that. We are outgunned by the opposition, and we had better take careful note of that fact before we proceed with this nonsensical approach to ending abortion. We are faced with conditions which indicate that mere political pressure will not get the job done. Look back at those conditions that I ended Chapter 1 with. The political and economic conditions dictate that we had better change strategy.

If you are getting the impression that I am not impressed with the actions being taken so far, you are right. I am distressed and frustrated by the lack of commitment, and at the same time I am impressed that so many have remained loyal to the cause in the face of much inner turmoil and conflict amongst pro-lifers. The road of the pro-lifer is indeed lonely. Every path seems to offer more frustration and turmoil. Dead end after dead end, apathy upon apathy, struggle after struggle, and progress seems so minimal. Yet, we go on, we fight on, and someday we believe that we will win. But, while believing we will win, there is that nagging doubt. We know we must win, but how? If I were to say we are desperate, that would be true. At this point, the future of the pro-life movement seems dim. It is not enough to want to win or deserve to win; we need to know how to win.

There is of recent date a new and solid hope to alter the law through the Supreme Court itself. That body is changing rapidly with the recent appointment of a new Chief Justice and also the appointment of a conservative replacement for that individual. Both men are opposed to abortion. It is ironic that the very body that brought about abortion on demand may be the quickest hope to ending it. That is far from certain, however, for no man is granted unending life on this earth, and the next Court appointment may be made to replace a conservative judge rather than a liberal one. It is also rather dubious because the next appointment may not be made by as conservative a President as Ronald Reagan is. If the next appointment made replaces a conservative judge, at best we gain no ground. We could lose ground if the new appointment is a liberal judge. If a liberal is replaced with a conservative, there is an excellent chance that the law will be affected. How long a process that would be or how it will unfold is a great uncertainty. In any case, it will take a long time for the entire process to work itself out.

The problem of putting our hopes upon the Supreme Court is that there is little certainty in that trust. There are simply too many unknowns. While the Supreme Court seems to offer much more hope for a resolution than Congress, it cannot be counted upon to end the conflict. Even if it does allow the states the right to regulate abortion, there will result a very long and intense struggle to end abortion that will then slip down to individual states. We will end up with some states protecting life and others not. Thus, we will have made abortion a bit more difficult for some, but for others we will have made no difference. No, there has to be a better solution: a solution that can be grasped even by liberals, and doesn't leave women's rights out of the picture; a solution that will rally many women who are now pro-abortion to the pro-life cause; a solution that is so effective that there is not an effective strategy to block it; a solution that will enable Congress to act and act decisively to call for an end to abortion in America. I know this sounds too good to be true, but the solution is awaiting the pro-life camp to grasp and utilize for the cause. Let me say that again. Such a solution already exists. We just need to rally behind it.

The purpose of this book is to present that solution to you. I will present what it is and how it must be instituted. How quickly it is accomplished will depend upon you and others like you who are able to grasp the significance of what is being said here and then act upon that significance. Please read the next chapters very carefully. They could change the very course of American history, even world history. I believe they will. I believe we have the ultimate victory well within our grasp. I pray that you come to believe as I do. Believing will not be enough, however. We must act, and act decisively. That will require courage. May God bless you with such courage!

FOUR

The Voice
of Rachel

Abortion is a horrible word. It means to terminate, to sever. Whenever we think of an abortion we have to think about two people: a mother and her baby. Oh, we may use cloaking techniques to disguise one, such as calling the baby "fetal tissue" or "a blob" or the "product of conception," but we are all quite aware that what we are talking about is a baby. While it is true that it is small and helpless, it is still a baby. The word fetus is often used, but insofar as it is used in an attempt to reduce the humanity of the unborn child we should not use it. *Fetus* is a term that is used to describe a stage of human development, not a stage of humanity. It is usually meant to describe the development, in the womb, of a baby from eight weeks to the end of pregnancy. We use other terms to describe other stages of development such as *baby, child, teenager, adult, senior citizen.* All of these describe a particular stage of development that a human goes through, and none of these is meant to make the subject either more or less human than the others.

Just as obviously, pregnancy does not define a different human woman, but a woman in a particular biological state. She is with child. It does not tell us if the child is a boy or a girl or if the child is one week or thirty weeks of age. It only describes a state of physical being. The point is that within the woman's body is a unique individual who is growing daily to arrive at an important stage of development called birth. Birth is not a magical day when suddenly the child in the womb becomes something unique from what it was; it is merely the day that the child changes its environment and is born. Biologically there is no change, except for the fact that now this tiny being is functioning independently of, but still very dependently upon, its mother and other human beings. There is no self-respecting doctor, scientist, or textbook that would say that birth is a magical event that endows this little person with all new and surpassingly significant physical and psychological qualities. To even think that is utter and complete nonsense, and yet that is exactly the premise that abortion is being built upon.

Abortion proclaims that a child doesn't attain humanhood until that magical event called birth. The complete ridiculousness of that argument is obvious. If the child survives an attempted abortion, often great effort is taken to save that child. Suddenly, magically, what was defined as subhuman has taken on special qualities. It is now a person and deserves equal protection by the law. Any fool can see the complete idiocy of such a point of view, and yet that is exactly the basis for allowing abortions. We are saying to a women the following: "If you kill your baby before it is born, it is a legally acceptable practice called abortion. If you kill your baby after it is born, it is an illegal act called murder."

We used to laugh in history classes at some of the foolish ideas that ancient people maintained. They thought they were doing the proper thing, but the folly of their actions seemed so obvious that it was difficult to understand how they could ever behave the way they did. Think of all the things that we take for granted now that would have been laughed at not that many years past! The reason for our gain is that we have been able to overcome ignorance. We simply didn't realize the magnificence of the creation around us. You would like to believe that with these advances has come enlightenment as well, but the opposite seems to be the case. We have entered a very strange age where we are making rapid technical and scientific advances while at the same time we are degenerating spiritually. Scientifically we are advancing very rapidly, and spiritually we are becoming barbarians.

We stand on the threshold of unimaginable advances and cling tenaciously to ignorant prejudices. To abort a child in the womb is to go against everything we know about this life and its humanity. Our practice of abortion is like seeking medical help from a witch doctor rather than a physician. I know of no greater act of moral cowardice than what is taking place in abortuaries across this land. Future generations will look at our monumental ignorance and shake their heads in disbelief. How can we be so stupid, so blind?

The result of all this is the tragic destruction of one and one-half million babies each year since the Supreme Court opened the floodgates in 1973—floodgates that the witch doctors of our society have fought savagely to keep open; floodgates that have swept the lives of the innocent into pools of blood while the draculean industry that sucks their lifeblood away thrives; floodgates the witch doctors have maintained are necessary because women must have their rights.

It turns my stomach when I hear their screeching voices rallying women and men to their cause. By them the unsuspecting, the innocent, the desperate, the weak, and the burdened are led down a path of sure and certain destruction. They, like their ancient counterpart the Devil, lie, distort, exaggerate, confuse, and corrupt all that we cherish as right and good. The malignancy of their cancerous presence destroys thousands upon thousands of innocent babies, unsuspecting mothers, and even an entire nation.

The surviving victims—the women—of which there are millions, are left helpless and crippled with nothing. They receive neither support nor condemnation from society. They are left in a horrifying void. These predatory creatures are sowing the seeds of their own destruction, and that is the key to their demise. Their malignancy will require exposure, complete and sure. When that happens, perhaps we can find a way to perform an operation that will eradicate their disease.

If I sound angry, I am, but I am not near as angry as their victims. It is on the victims, the surviving victims, that we must center our attention if we are to understand that abortion can be defeated, along with its proponents. It will take careful and wise action to do so. The pro-abortionists have implanted an unstoppable force in their midst, and all that it will take for that force to turn on them is for us to unleash it. We can win the war, and it will not be as difficult as one would imagine.

In the Book of Jeremiah (31:15) we have the following words recorded:

> A voice was heard in Ramah, weeping and great mourning, Rachel weeping for her children; and she refused to be comforted, because they were no more.

When the words appear in Jeremiah they are words of prophecy—words about a time when there would be a great slaughter of children and for whom there would be uncontrolled mourning. Scripture makes it clear that a fulfillment of that prophecy took place when Herod ordered the destruction of all male children two years of age and under in an attempt to kill the baby Jesus. Many prophecies have several fulfillments, and I believe that this is one that also is relevant to this age. In fact, there is little denying that it is. Whether you believe this is a fulfillment of Scripture or not, the substance of what the prophet said is now true. Today, there is the voice of weeping and great mourning as the modern-day Rachel weeps for her children, for they are no more.

There is an organization that has arisen in the United States and which has now branched into other countries called WEBA, which means Women Exploited By Abortion. The women of WEBA all testify that they have had an abortion. Thus, they are not removed from what we are talking about. They are women who are able to provide firsthand testimony of the evil effects abortion has had on their life. They know how much abortion has damaged them, and they are dedicated to preventing other women from having to go through the same agony. They have devoted themselves to reaching out to other women who are suffering as they have and need someone who cares and understands. They are modern Rachels weeping for their children.

Before I get into WEBA and its role in the destruction of abortion, I want to relate to you some information about women and abortion that is very true and important to remember. Very few women will admit that they have had an abortion. Abortion is not a fact that a woman wants to have associated with herself. She will talk about abortion and whether or not she is for or against it, but very few wish to be identified with the experience of having had an abortion.

I realize that there will always be exceptions. When you are dealing with so many women you will always find exceptions. A tiny minority of women swear that their abortion was the greatest thing they could have done. I believe such women are too often the ones the press gravitates to and then proclaims, "See, women have abortions, and they come through it just fine!" What it is doing is helping create an illusion that a woman can have an abortion and simply dismiss the whole thing as a simple, safe procedure which has very few side effects. The baby is kept out of the picture because that subject presents some very uncomfortable areas to delve into. Keep it a piece of tissue and therefore a non-entity.

I also know, from direct conversations with such women, that many women who once applauded their abortion as wonderful now deeply regret what they did. What they once thought was a life-saving operation is now a life-threatening fact with which they will have to live for the rest of their lives. Their lives were fine for years with no noticeable effects of the abortion occupying their minds, and then suddenly everything began to go wrong. Abortion is not a simple procedure that once done will remain hidden in the recesses of a woman's mind never to reappear. Eventually it will surface and usually in a very destructive manner. The direct known effects of abortion can take place years after the actual abortion. When you understand that, you begin to understand the problem that we are facing.

There are several important factors at work here. First, the fact that she decided to end the life of her child. That fact cannot and will not be altered by using false terminology. Call the child or baby anything you wish, but the woman who is with child knows within herself she is carrying a live human being. Telling her sweet lies to comfort her at the time of the abortion and, naturally, as a persuasion to have the abortion does not alter the fact that she knows, deep within herself, that she is taking a life that she has no right to take.

The abortion industry is the most dirty, rotten industry in the world, for not only does it murder innocent children, but it also robs women of a peaceful life. The abortion experience will come back to haunt women until all of the peace they thought they once had will be replaced with despair. This filthy industry spews out lies in order to maintain its iron grip upon women so that it can devour their children and get paid a handsome sum in the process. Abortionists and those who are their assistants, such as nurses, and those who feed the women to them such as Planned Parenthood, clergy, and physicians, most of whom wouldn't perform the abortion themselves but send their patients to the butchers, are the real scum of our society. If ever there was a group of people that is destroying this society, it is this group.

As a clergyman, I seethe with anger at those Judas figures who hide behind the cleric but have no conception of the Lord whom they are falsely representing. I call for them to admit that they do not stand upon one Biblical principle and to turn in their collars, for they are not fit to be called Christian. I do not pass judgment upon them; that is the province of Almighty God, and He will judge them in due time. I wish I could say of them that they know not what they do, but that would be a lie. God have mercy upon them.

Shakespeare wrote a wonderful play called *Macbeth*. The story centers on the life of Macbeth and his wife. Witches have told Macbeth that he will be king. As we are prone to do in life, he and his wife attempt to bring about their own destiny. They resort to murdering the king to get him out of their way—after all, he blocks their path to happiness, and once he is removed they are convinced the witches' promise will be fulfilled. Then they will have the happiness they have begun to desperately seek, the happiness the witches have convinced them they deserve. The murder has a predictably disastrous effect—it plunges them into ruin. Their deception was the product of their own wishful thinking rather than truth. They both suffer extreme mental anguish as Lady Macbeth becomes insane and Macbeth watches his dreams and hopes melt into oblivion. It is a sad tragedy, but a prophetic picture of what happens to anyone who attempts to allow the end to justify the means.

The siren song of the abortionist camp is that there is a need for abortion so that women and men in our society can have the happiness they deserve. They should not be burdened by an unwanted child. The argument is accepted by desperate women who believe they cannot possibly raise the child, that the child is a threat to their happiness. A woman's fears are used against her to persuade her that the life that she takes will affect her no more than having a tooth filled. This baby stands in the path to happiness. It must be removed so that the ultimate goal of personal fulfillment is achieved.

These desperate women begin to believe that what they will do is both acceptable and good. List after list of rational reasons are put forth as to why the child must die, and finally when they have believed enough of those lies, they commit the act of murder. They were, in fact, very easy prey for the abortionist. They really didn't want to face the truth at that moment anymore than the abortionist wants to tell them the truth. Instead of the truth, the abortionist tells them lies—cold, plain, deliberate lies: "It is only a blob of tissue." "It doesn't even look like a human baby." "It's not human yet." "This won't hurt." "It's perfectly safe." Whatever it takes, and usually that isn't much, it's soon all over. Some money is exchanged. The quick procedure is carried out. The woman goes home void of the life that was growing within her. Somewhere deep within her there is a very sick, gnawing feeling that it isn't over, it's just begun. In truth, the horror that she is going to face has only begun.

Let me say something to you, and please be sure that you understand this. I am not talking about the exception, I am talking about the norm. This is what happens in the majority of cases involving abortion. We are taking the life of nearly one and one-half million babies each year, and we are ruthlessly destroying the lives of an equally great number of women. Moreover, I haven't even mentioned the fathers, grandparents, brothers and sisters, and concerned members of society, for whom the loss is painfully real. Abortion is creating a nation of broken people who are living with the hell that a child, a beautiful unknown child, is dead because they deliberately killed it. Some of those individuals know they are directly responsible for that murder, and that fact is nearly impossible for them to live with.

Our nation is filled with fathers who have watched their wife or girlfriend destroy their baby and who had absolutely no choice in the matter. They could plead, they could cry, they could beg that the killing not take place, but they had no legal right to interfere. The ultimate decision is in the hands of the mother, and she is being persuaded to kill her child. Our nation is filled with people who have to view the horror of abortion as it goes on around them and be told that it is not their business, that they should not be concerned. They have no right to save an innocent human life. America is on a collision course with itself, and the results of that collision will not be pretty.

I believe there is a greater degree of suffering going on

in America than there has ever been before. In fact, this is happening around the world, where abortion is accepted as the standard. We live in a world that has gone insane over its own ability to control through killing. While I will concern myself only with the United States, the same things are happening in the rest of the world. A nation cannot kill its children and remain free and great. America is truly on the road of self-destruction. It is rotting from within, and no matter how soothing the voices of the pro-abortionist camp may sound, their call is a siren call to destruction. We must silence them, or face the reality that they will lead to the total and complete destruction of all that we love and cherish.

What I am describing is happening all around us. We are losing the very basis of our freedom in a land that was formed so that everyone could enjoy life, liberty, and the pursuit of happiness. This has become a lie. Our moral fiber is locked hopelessly into the lie that that which is legal is moral. We go on killing babies at the rate of more than four thousand each day. We go on multiplying the carnage. We go on believing the lies that arise out of greed. We go on and on with the nightmare while the few voices that have arisen to warn about the senselessness of it all and of the impending danger have been laughed to scorn. All the while a voice is heard in Ramah, Rachel weeping for her children, and she refuses to be comforted, for they are no more. In those prophetic words are the key that will help us to end abortion. In the next chapter we will look closely at WEBA and the impact it can have upon this issue. We are on the road to finding the end to abortion, and it is a solution that needs to be fully understood.

FIVE

A New Force
For Life

I began to mention a specific group in Chapter 4, and it is a group that I wish to discuss in more detail. I refer to WEBA, Women Exploited By Abortion. As I said, these women all testify that they have had an abortion. They are individuals who have gone through the abortion experience, rather who are going through the abortion experience, but have a distinct difference from other women in the same situation. They have found something that has changed their life. They have found healing in Jesus Christ. They have faced the sobering consequences of their selfish action and realized that there is but one way to rid themselves of years of anguish and guilt, and that is at the feet of the Savior. Before I go into that, let me back up a bit.

I call the abortionists liars. I do so on the basis of the evidence that these women have presented. It is the exceptional woman—in fact, I have yet to find one—who will tell you that the doctor or the abortion clinic counselors told her the truth about the baby she was carrying or about the possible consequences of the abortion she was about to have. These women were told that it was a simple procedure which would soon be over with and forgotten. What they were told was not only not the truth, but a purposeful, damnable lie! I know it makes your stomach churn to think about it, but the truth is that these doctors and clinics make their money by aborting the baby, not by counseling women to keep their babies. There is no money in that. They don't tell the truth because the truth is bad for business. So they purposely lie. I can present woman after woman who will testify to the truth of what I have just said. Here are a few quotes:

> The doctor said a little fluid out and some fluid injected, severe cramps and then the fetus is expelled. That isn't what it was. I felt my girl thrash around for an hour and a half until she died a slow death. I had hard labor for over 12 hours and delivered my daughter myself. She was beautiful . . . but dead at five and one half months.

> My doctor didn't tell me about the possible profuse bleeding and infection that lasted for weeks. And he never said anything about the possibility of the hysterectomy I had to have eight months later.

> No one told me I would live with this decision for the rest of my life. It's been several years, but my grief continues.

I could go on and on and on with different and sadly similar stories of women who should have been and deserved to have been told the truth, but weren't. The result has been that they have paid dearly for what they most likely would not have done if they had been told the sobering consequences of abortion. I have talked to women who have had abortions over ten years ago, and they still cry, weep and mourn. The hurt doesn't go away; it only intensifies. These women are hurting, and their hurt is not erased by lies. They know the truth, and wish it were not so. They know the truth and wish they had been told it much sooner, when there was still a chance of saving the life they so carelessly ended. Their story is sad and tragic. I weep when I talk to them, I bleed for them in my heart. I wish there was a way for them to erase the awful memory of what they did and what was done to them. For most of them it may truly be said, "Father, forgive them, for they didn't know what they were doing."

If there is an effective way to end abortion in America, these women are the key. If we are going to destroy this godless act of brutality, then we must mobilize the most potentially damaging force we can muster that is available, and it is available in these women. These women are the internal key that will cause the abortion industry to have to face up to the fact that it is a dirty business run by ruthless individuals who have truly exploited women for personal gain. A house divided against itself cannot stand, and these women are an open sore in the abortionist industry's side. They are the thing the abortionist fears the most, a living, active victim. Their numbers are probably close to the number of babies aborted each year. What they are to the pro-life cause is living victims who are more than willing to lend their aid and counsel to destroy that which destroyed their peace and the baby they now wish they could call back from the grave. The abortionist, except through denial and further lies, is helpless against this foe, for no tyrant can long stand against his victims when they unite together to overthrow him.

WEBA states that in practically every case they have documented, the woman was never really given all of the facts. Many times abortion was described as clinically safe, and no explanation of the damage this "safe" procedure could inflict was given. Here are some established effects of abortion.

Physical effects include the following: sterility, miscarriages, ectopic pregnancies, stillbirths, menstrual disturbances, bleeding, infections, shock, coma, perforated uterus, peritonitus, passing blood clots, fever/cold sweats, intense pain, loss of other organs, crying, insomnia, loss of appetite, weight loss, exhaustion, nervousness, decreased work capacity, vomiting, gastro-intestinal disturbances, and frigidity.

The psychological effects include: guilt, suicidal impulses, sense of loss, unfulfillment, mourning, regret, remorse, withdrawal, loss of confidence, low self-esteem, pre-occupation with death, hostility, self-destructive behavior, anger, rage, helplessness, rememberance of death date, pre-occupation with "due date," intense interest in babies, thwarted maternal instincts, loss of sexual drive, inability to forgive, dehumanization of self, nightmares, seizures and tremors, frustration, feelings of being exploited, and child abuse.

The physical effects can be immediate, but not always. They can be a direct result of the psychological effects. What actually takes place is a sadly twisted interplay of the physical and psychological side effects that were probably always there, but were suppressed until triggered by something that intensified their presence. For some women the effects were exposed dramatically when they became pregnant with another child. For some just seeing a baby causes deep hurt and triggers the release of pent-up emotion. It can be any number of things, but the fact remains that the result is very destructive.

Some women turn to illicit sexual relationships, drugs, alcohol, and any number of self-destructive measures. Often, and here is part of the tragic problem, they don't make the immediate connection between what is happening to them and the abortion experience. They don't realize that the abortion they thought they handled very well is exploding inside of them. Their life is being destroyed and they don't know why.

The story of too many women, in fact most, is hidden. Their lives are being wrecked, and society doesn't realize that the cause is in plain sight. Without exception, the women who have come forth and talked about their abortion experience have displayed some of the symptoms described above. They found themselves totally unequipped to deal with the result of what was hoped would be a termination of a real problem in their life. What they discovered is that although the child was removed, what remained was more serious. In truth, it was left inside them but in a different way. The mother, instead of being released from an unwanted pregnancy, was placed into a position where she was unable to free herself from the child she sought to destroy. That child is destroyed physically, but the psychological aftereffects are almost impossible to deal with. There is a "ghost" that keeps presenting itself, and that ghost causes nightmare experiences.

As one woman put it:

> If only I had the courage to give it a chance. But I didn't take the time to think it through—I just panicked and it was as if I had awoken from a terrible nightmare to find my baby gone, Michael gone, and nothing left but shame and guilt, and a kind of overpowering remorse that can only be felt by someone who had everything, and then selfishly, impulsively, threw it all away.

Some women go out and buy a cemetery plot. There is no body, but it helps them to handle the grief. Some celebrate the "birth date," and many have named their child. The celebration of the birth date cannot be regarded as a joyous event. It is a day of mourning. Often the "birth day" is really the death date or the date the child would have been born. Tragic? Yes, but it's happening to millions of women across the land. Unless something is done, it will go on happening. Something has to be done to stop the killing. Something has to be done to end the conflict and mental torment.

This is not an easy subject for me to deal with. I have seen the grief of too many women. I am thankful that I have never heard the other scream, the scream of the child that momentarily survived an abortion. Some women have heard their child scream that way, and it will torment their soul as long as they live. Regardless, that scream is there, deep within my soul. I know it as a scream for help, and I know that if there is anything decent in my soul, I must answer that cry. My heart bleeds for the child that is never given a chance to live. My heart bleeds for the mother that had been given one of God's most precious gifts and then refused it.

I have always felt that one of the characteristics of barbarian people is that they don't have a basic respect for life. They might be the most advanced nation in every respect, but still be barbaric. What else can you call a nation whose people are educated and know the truth, but who choose to ignore it? What is a fitting term for a nation that kills its babies and calls it the furtherance of human rights? What do you call a nation that rejoices over the right to commit savagery and to do it by its best-educated and most-respected members, the medical profession? What do you call a nation that refuses to hear the cries for mercy? What do you call a nation that will not have pity on its most weak and innocent members?

The Apostle Paul asked the Galatians, "Who bewitched you?" Who bewitched our nation? The Galatians had turned their back on life and embraced death. When the Supreme Court refused to protect the most innocent life in our midst, it too turned its back on life and embraced death. Perhaps *bewitched* is the term that is fitting our nation and people. It helps explain actions that run counter to reason. *Bewitched* explains the mesmerizing effect that the abortionist has had on this land.

Only an evil that runs very deep and strong would be able to persuade a woman to destroy her child and pay to have it done. Only Satan could get women to self-destruct and at the same time convince them this is a wonderful right that they must protect at all costs. One thing we can always count on Satan for: he is a liar. When he does tell the truth, it is to support a lie. There is one thing, other than the living God, that he hates, and that is the truth. He has good reason to fear, for his cruel and beastly ways are being exposed in the light of truth. Hopefully, someone will listen before it is too late for them as well. We have to break his spell, and the truth, the undeniable truth, will do it. We have to free the women in bondage. The blood of Jesus Christ, and the forgiveness it offers, will set them free.

Catherine Ann Speckhard, a Ph.D. from the University of Minnesota, published a study of the long-term effects of abortion upon women. Her studies confirmed what a great many of us knew all along. Some of the things she found were as follows:

- 81 percent reported a preoccupation with the aborted child.
- 73 percent reported flashbacks of the abortion experience.
- 69 percent reported feelings of craziness after the abortion.
- 54 percent recalled nightmares related to the abortion.
- 35 percent had perceived visitations from the aborted child.
- 23 percent reported hallucinations related to the abortion.
- 96 percent in retrospect regarded abortion as the taking of a human life—as murder.
- 72 percent of these women, who were from diverse backgrounds, said they had no religious beliefs of substance at the time of their abortion.

These were the effects studied in women who had their abortion from five to ten years ago. Time is called the great healer, but it is evident that time alone is not able to heal the effects of abortion on women.

The picture that a study of this sort paints of women who have had an abortion has to be sobering. Millions of women have had an abortion. Millions of women are suffering. Behind it all is one of the most devious cover-ups of all time, and the reason for the cover-up is that we are dealing with strong and politically powerful organizations. Part of the problem is that the effects of abortions aren't always linked to the abortion experience. Part of the problem is that we don't want to admit that we have a problem. Part of the problem is that we don't want to admit that we live in a country that has ceased to care. Part of the problem is that if we admit what we have done, how can we live with the guilt? A big part of the problem is that most people simply don't care. Apathy is rampant in America, and where apathy is strong, justice is difficult.

Yet, there are women who are coping with the realization of their own failure. There are women who are dealing with the tragedy of the death they helped bring about. These women are certainly in the minority, but someday thousands, perhaps millions, will join their ranks and be given the help they need. The suffering millions of men who have seen their child destroyed can turn to this same source of strength as can grandparents and a host of others who suffer because of this deadly plague in our midst.

That is what WEBA is all about. WEBA exists to bring the healing of Christ to wounded hearts. It is there to offer the support so badly needed by suffering women. WEBA is an organization dedicated to helping expose the horrors of abortion, to be sure, but it is there to help those victims of abortion that have nowhere to turn. WEBA is an organization of love, for their love is one which offers help and healing, not empty promises or damaging lies. The WEBA women are frank, because that is what they needed in the first place but didn't get.

Listen to a WEBA woman:

After my abortion in 1969, I was so filled with regret, remorse, and self-recrimination that I became anorexic and nearly starved myself to death. When my weight dropped below 80 pounds and I developed a potentially fatal heart condition (at 20 years of age!) I was hospitalized. I spent 32 weeks in the psychiatric unit of a hospital where I had a series of shock treatments and learned to appreciate the emotional anesthesia induced by certain prescription drugs. Upon my release I began to abuse drugs, then alcohol. Several years passed during which time I was treated for drug overdoses, and I attempted suicide twice. I married but was so emotionally ill I could not sustain a relationship. After only a month my husband left me.

It was apparent that unless there was a supernatural force outside of me that could order my life far better than I could, my life would never be worth living. I had tried astrology and other occult religions to no avail. Finally, in utter despair and desperation, I turned to God. In the early hours of a morning that followed an anguished night, I fell on my knees and cried out, "If there is a God, and if He cares for me, I beg Him to do something to ease my hurt and straighten out my life." What followed was a miracle. Somewhere deep inside of me I felt a sense of relief begin to grow. I sensed a warmth, a security such as a child feels when his mother washes his fevered brow with a cool cloth. Somehow I knew my life was going to be different from this time on.

And it was. My marriage was restored by God and now, nearly 10 years later, is strong and happy. I have three beautiful children and a productive, balanced life.

Jesus picked up the pieces of my life and put it back together again. Sure, sometimes I still grieve for my aborted child. I wonder what he (or she) would have been like and I sorrow that I denied myself the joy of nurturing him. But I know one thing for certain: someday soon when Jesus comes in the clouds of glory to claim the faithful of all ages, my child will be restored to me and I will be with him in the Place where there is no grief or death.

The testimony given above is not really all that different from thousands of others. Oh, there are unique pages in the life of every person, but one fact remains true in life after life: before these women met and accepted Jesus as their Lord and Savior they were in a horrible mess and their life was slowly being destroyed by something which they could not handle. Any life out of control is a life that is not in the Savior's hands. Abortion puts lives out of control.

Nothing can make what has been done in an abortion right except the forgiveness and love of the Savior. Psychologists and counselors who attempt to help a woman without the forgiveness and healing of Jesus Christ are not helping her. They are putting off the healing that can be hers by attempting methods that are not effective in dealing with the needs that she has at this moment in her life. She is filled with a tremendous amount of grief, and that grief will not be satisfied by anything short of the comfort of the cross.

I realize that there will be many people who will disagree with those words. The non-Christian world is an enemy of the cross of Christ and does not see the need for the Savior's forgiveness. That is a fact that we in the pro-life movement must recognize as more than a difference in philosophy or attitude; it is a hard fact that must be dealt with.

Abortion is sin. Until you accept that fact you will never be able to understand that what a woman needs most at this time in her life is release from the guilt and burden of sin. To call something sin when it truly is, is not being unkind. It is being honest. What a woman who has had an abortion needed from the outset was honesty. She didn't receive it and as a result, her child is dead. That is what dishonesty does: it kills. To tell her now that what she is experiencing is not the result of sin is another lie. It will be no benefit to her, but will continue to do her great harm.

Many in the pro-life movement are not Christian. There is a great amount of pressure to keep Christ out of the movement, for it is feared that this will weaken our position rather than strengthen it. That is utter and complete nonsense. When David faced Goliath he did so because God was with him. If God hadn't been, David would have died and not Goliath. If we in the pro-life movement don't come to realize that we need God, and still wish to be victorious, we will end up whipped and shattered. WEBA recognizes that fact, and its members have a clear understanding that healing comes not from men but from Christ.

A woman needs to hear forgiveness spoken directly to her. She needs to forgive herself and those who did such a horrible deed to her. She needs to feel the love and support of those who have felt as she has and who have come out of the abortion experience with healing and hope. She needs to be able to talk openly and frankly about her feelings and emotions, especially in regard to the child that she misses so much. The last point is the most difficult for her, for it is a step that brings her out to a very vulnerable position.

In WEBA she will find herself surrounded by women who have experienced what she has, women who love her and are concerned about who she is and what has happened to her. She will find sisters who really care about her. She will never forget the child that she lost, but she will learn to forgive herself and those who did the killing as well as to experience that beautiful peace that comes through knowing Christ as her Savior. She can begin to live again, and perhaps in time she can become a vital part of the movement to end abortion. She can become a source of strength to others.

Of course, there are support groups in churches that are also helping to fill the role that WEBA is filling. The church can help, but only if it is openly opposed to abortion and sensitive to the hurts suffered by a woman who has experienced the loss of a child to this killer. If the church does not recognize the healing love of the Savior, it cannot offer the woman much more than the world. The church does lack the one element so vital to this ministry, and that is peer support as offered by a group such as WEBA. I am sure that there are some churches that are offering this ministry, but sad to say, they are few in number. If a church really wants to help, it should explore the possibility of supporting a WEBA chapter, that is, if there is one in your community. Don't, and I emphasize, don't attempt to start a WEBA chapter that is directly connected with your church. A woman who is suffering is often in great fear of the church and what it will do. She needs to have a "safe" haven. Your church may be a very safe haven for her to turn to, but she doesn't trust that. You can and must get your church to openly condemn abortion as well as to make it clear that the complete forgiveness of Christ is available to any person that

77

has had one and is truly repentant of her action. There will be ample opportunity to minister to such women as they grow out of their shell.

WEBA is important because it assists these women to talk about the problems they face. It provides an outlet for their anger and grief. It gives them an opportunity to get into the fight to save lives, and it continues to minister to women long after others have failed.

I did not mean to ignore the other victims of abortion, the father, the grandparents, the siblings, and the mass of people who grieve because abortion exists in this country. The need that they have is very much the same as the woman who has had an abortion. Fathers, especially those who urged the abortion decision, need forgiveness and love. They need Christ. Some of these men are deeply hurting.

A while ago I heard the owner of an abortion clinic addressing a group of college students make jest of a man who picketed her clinic. Her description of him was of a lunatic who constantly showed up on days when abortions were going to be performed. He dressed in a cape and carried on with tears and pleas to women entering the clinic to stop and spare their baby. She laughed at him before the group and said that this was the typical nut that she had to put up with. The class enjoyed her caricature. What she did not relate to the class was the fact that his wife had had an abortion at her clinic, and he had begged her to spare their child's life. The tragedy had left him overcome with grief. Some fathers cannot bear the grief of having their baby butchered. They have no recourse under the law, and often the mother will not listen to their pleas to spare the child. The mother has the right to kill the child. Some men can handle that and some can't. I believe that more can't than we imagine.

WEBA women tell me that they get many calls from grandparents, especially women, who are grieving because their daughter or daughter-in-law had an abortion and killed their grandchild. These people suffer too. They need the healing love of Jesus Christ. Nothing else will do. Only Christ can set them free.

The list of victims goes on and on. We actually don't know how many people are affected with the taking of human life. We do know that there is always at least one other life beside the child affected, and the total number of these is a staggering figure. Something has to be done and now. Abortion will not do anything but destroy. It can never heal. In the next chapter we are going to explore more about the Pro-Life Manifesto, and what it is. WEBA is a key part of that manifesto. It is because WEBA is dedicated to Christ.

One last word about WEBA. The women of WEBA need your support. I mean money and encouragement. They need to know that you understand what they are facing and that you want to help. In Chapter 12 I list their national address. Write them and don't forget to include a check. Non-profit organizations don't get very many breaks with expenses. To get the word out about WEBA and what it is doing to help women, and men, is expensive. If you care, help.

SIX

The Way to Victory

The war that is going on over abortion rights is a war that is peculiar in many respects. Its peculiar nature stems from the fact that it is a war over ideologies centered around rights. One side is fighting very hard to protect the rights of the baby. They have been dealt a severe blow from the Supreme Court which declared that the baby in the womb had no rights. It even declared that state governments didn't have the right to disagree with their opinion. Although women have failed to admit it, they were dealt a severe blow when that same Supreme Court decided in 1986 that doctors had no obligation to explain the hazards of abortion to women who were seeking an abortion. Thus, they could perform a very hazardous operation, the long-range effects of which there is ample evidence to indicate are very damaging, and give no accounting to the recipient of that operation, even if that information is requested by the woman as a basis of making her decision as to whether or not to have an abortion.

What this suggests is that the women's rights groups have gotten paranoid about abortion and its protection as a right in that they even view a law that would give women the right to basic information about what is happening to their person as being threatening to their rights! What seems to be taking place is that the means has become so important that even the end has been lost in its wake. Thus, the right to have abortions unrestricted has become more important to them than even the right to make a well-informed decision. Unless I am misunderstanding something, wasn't that what this whole issue was about, the right of a woman to make a sound, well-informed decision which was right for her? Instead, we have the woman being coerced into abortion, irrespective of her personal needs or choice. Obviously, anytime we put our lives into the hands of anyone, we should have the right to know what the consequences of their action will be. If the decision were over any other matter, and if the Court handed down a decision like *Thornburgh vs. ACOG,* which struck down a Pennsylvania informed consent law, I am convinced that the women's groups would have been enraged! It ran directly counter to all that they have attempted to accomplish for so many years, and yet they hailed it as a victory. The only possible explanation is that they have lost their ability to reason when it comes to the issue of abortion.

Paranoia can be defined as "well-rationalized delusions of persecution or grandeur." The key to understanding paranoia is that the delusions are well-rationalized. Thus, when women began to hail the 1986 Supreme Court decision that was actually robbing them of rights, it was based upon the false assumption that this thwarted an attempt by pro-lifers to rob them of some rights. Thus, a defeat for them became a victory because it was perceived as a defeat for the pro-life forces. The Supreme Court was hailed as a champion because it frustrated the pro-life forces by knocking down an attack against women. If they would have been rational in their thinking they would have realized that the law that was knocked down wasn't a threat to women's rights. It may have prevented many abortions, but was also an attempt to insure that when a woman made the choice to abort her baby, it would be an informed choice.

The real threat was to the abortionist, not to the woman's rights movement. Since there is a perception among ultra-liberal women that abortionists are their friends and allies, they took the law as being a direct attack upon them.

The threat to the abortionist was that he was going to lose money. For if the truth is made known as to what abortion is, most women will refuse to have one. If the law had been upheld and the abortionists continued to withhold the truth, they would have been in jeopardy of lawsuits arising out of damages resulting from normal abortions.

The woman's rights movement of the liberal camp has thrown a tremendous amount of weight behind abortion. They see it as a vital issue for them to back. It is no small coincidence that organizations such as NOW, Planned Parenthood, and NARAL continue to urge women to make that association. These organizations in particular, and there are more, survive because of abortion. It is in their best interest to insure that the woman's rights movement does not dissociate itself with the abortion issue. For the moment at least, they seem to have no fear that that will happen.

What is almost forgotten is that there are national organizations for women that view abortion as wrong. These organizations, such as Eagle Forum, put their emphasis upon protecting the rights of all members of society. They have seen clearly that abortion is not an answer to our problems, but that it is creating new and greater problems. I bring up such organizations because they demonstrate very clearly that women can work for rights and decency in society and not have to endorse abortion as a necessity for women.

All of this is mentioned because it is clear to many individuals that the war cannot be won the way it is currently being waged. Ideologies are not changed by protesting or marching or picketing or education. I am not saying that these aren't good and necessary; they lay groundwork, but they do not change hearts. The picketers in front of a hospital or abortion clinic are making a public statement. They are saying that there are citizens in this country that view abortion as murder and that they want the killing to stop. When large groups of people are gathered together to march, they are making a public statement that there are people who will not cease from their efforts until their cause is established. The education process is designed to reach the uncommitted to show them the reason for the concern. All of these work together, but none will end the war.

On the political front, it seems very obvious that the pro-life and the pro-abortion camps have some heavy hardware for lobbying. Politicians are playing games with both forces and using them to fatten campaign coffers. While there are some very committed congressmen, many are sitting in a position where they are hoping that they can keep straddling the fence. While the pro-abortion camp is well funded, the pro-life camp isn't. Thus, the pro-life camp really can't afford to get into a votes war. While there are claims of progress in turning the Senate or House, in actuality it seems very unlikely that mere campaigning will do the trick. The pro-life camp just does not have the clout that will make, indeed force, politicians to listen. Every election we see millions of our badly needed resources go down the drain to politicians who either don't get elected or who turn their back on us once elected. We get lip service, but very little action. The 1986 elections have clearly shown how worthless a pro-life political strategy can be. We are as blind in that thinking as the pro-abortionists are in believing that abortion must be preserved at all costs. We are now anxiously awaiting the next election in the hopes of making a dent in the pro-abortionist camp. The fact remains that in two years we will gain little ground and have lost three million babies in the process. We simply lack adequate leadership in the pro-life camp, and until we get leadership with vision and understanding of the strategy needed to win, we will continue to lose.

Should we give up trying to win elections? No! We must always attempt to elect congressmen that reflect our values. What I am saying is that merely attempting to win the pro-life cause by winning enough seats will not succeed. Yet, we are seeing that concept being pushed by one of the largest pro-life organizations in the United States. They, like their counterpart in the woman's rights camp, are filled with the delusion that they can legislate a moral issue. It simply can't be done, not because of the power of the opposition, but more importantly because that is not the way to do it. Ideology is not changed by law. It is changed by attacking the root of the matter, and that means that we have to find a way to disenchant women who are now firmly entrenched in the abortion rights cause. That is no easy task, for it takes a powerful message to get through the paranoia that develops in the protection of a cause. This is especially true because of the way that abortion is entrenched in the thinking of the women's rights camp. Abortion, to them, seems to hold the future for their further progress, and if the abortion cause is lost, so is the future. That is not reality, but remember, they are not dealing with reality. They are dealing with their own rationalized view of reality. Even if an argument is not based upon good solid evidence, many will flock to it if they have been convinced that it is necessary for their future good and that to accept the counterargument will spell loss for all that they have tried to accomplish. Sometimes it takes a very rude shock to drive the point home, and then, when minds have been set free from programmed thinking, conditions begin to change very rapidly.

To win the war for life, the pro-life camp has to develop a new strategy that does exactly what is needed to shock the pro-abortionist camp back to reality. To do that is a very difficult and delicate operation, but there is a way to get the job done. The reason that the pro-life camp will emerge victorious in this struggle is that there is no measure that I am aware of that the abortionists can use to disenchant the pro-life camp. We have the distinct advantage, but we had better learn how to use it. The result will be that women will be better off and babies in the womb will be safe. That is giving both sides a victory and bringing together two opposing forces to unite in a common goal. Women will emerge with more freedom and rights than ever before, and abortion will not be a part of it.

The evidence must be both irrefutable—although initially it will be challenged—and incontrovertible. There must be such a ground swell of opinion that even the most adamant of the opposing forces must begin to doubt their position. It must in fact have a villain, and in this case there isn't much difficulty in finding one, and it must offer the defeated as well as the victors the feeling that they have won. They must emerge together as fighting a common foe. They must emerge together as allies that have come to recognize a common evil. They must emerge together as being concerned about the same issues. A neat trick? Yes. Impossible? No!

That is the purpose of this Pro-Life Manifesto. It is to lay out the plan of attack that will do exactly what I have stated. We must direct our efforts in such a way that we cannot be defeated. In fact, the only thing that can beat us is apathy from within. Against that we have little power, but apathy too will be overcome with genuine concern. It does not matter that we broadcast what we are about, for there is no defense for what we will do. As long as there are abortions being performed, the other side is sowing the seeds of their own destruction. The strategy I am about to present is a winning strategy. Abortion will end, and women will win as well. That is the beauty of the Pro-Life Manifesto. There are no losers except one, the abortion industry and those connected with it.

The problem is not so much developing an effective strategy as it is getting the pro-life camp on board behind that strategy. That is the real difficulty. It is vital that the pro-life forces understand why they have failed and why they will continue to fail if they continue to pursue the present strategy. Pray that God will open the hearts and eyes of leadership within the pro-life camp! This is crucial. I might mention that the opposition has no problem in seeing the effectiveness of this strategy. That should be voice enough for what is being attempted.

The pro-life camp is badly divided. There are too many factions working against each other. They all believe that they alone have the answer to the abortion problem and sadly enough no one, alone, does. They are angry and suspicious of one another and believe that their efforts alone will produce victory. Unfortunately, none of them have a workable solution. Some of the ideas sound good on paper, but they don't work. What we are seeing is wasted time and energy for causes, no matter how well-intentioned, that will never succeed. They are wasting valuable resources and costing precious time. Time is precious to the pro-life camp, for every twenty seconds another baby dies. We don't have time to fool around with ineffective methods. We have to do it right, and we have to do it now. We need everyone dedicated to life to put their every effort into something that will work. The Pro-Life Manifesto is just that—it *will* work.

The first point of the Pro-Life Manifesto is that we must destroy abortion from within. It is not enough to show the horror that is done to the victim that dies. We must show clearly the horror to the victims that survive. To do that we must use our every resource to call forth the millions of victims of this modern-day holocaust to testify to the horror that abortion has been to their life. When we have literally millions of victims pointing the finger of accusation at the abortionists and decrying what abortion has done to them, both physically and mentally, people, including the press, will begin to listen. And when the press speaks, congressmen will listen. When Congress listens, the courts will listen and things will begin to change. Even diehard abortionists will listen, for they will have no choice. Please understand that until we have enough living victims opening the now-closed eyes and ears of a blind and deaf society, no one will see the torn bodies of the dead victims, the babies. They will simply refuse to, but they cannot ignore for long the cries and mourning of millions of women, for a woman's tears are more effective than dynamite in moving hardened hearts to compassion.

The strategy is simple, but unstoppable. It uses the obvious principle that if there is enough internal dissension, a movement will fail. We already know that the destructive force that exists within the abortion camp is powerful and ready to be unleashed. Abortion will explode if the right methods are applied to release the suffering, damaged women who trusted abortion to be an answer to their problems and found it to be a nightmare beyond their ability to cope.

The second principle of the Pro-Life Manifesto calls for all pro-life groups to begin to channel efforts into making this internal explosion happen. The sooner we get together and map a strategy for doing that, the sooner we will see abortion die. It cannot stand when literally millions of men and women are beginning to assail it for what it has done to their personal lives. These individuals grieve the loss of their babies. They are angry with the pro-abortionists, and that anger must be properly focused to put an end to the force that not only destroyed their peace and happiness but also killed their baby.

Up till now our divisions have been our downfall. Cooperation has not been our strongest point. We each seem content to pursue our own little pro-life empires. That nonsense must stop. Certainly there are things that are being done that are important, but they must be secondary to the primary objective which is the internal explosion of the abortion camp. It is up to the members of the various pro-life groups to get that point clearly across to their leadership.

The Pro-Life Manifesto calls for immediate and powerful efforts to help break the silence of fear that surrounds the women and men who have suffered through the self-abasing act of abortion. The pro-life camp must become a center for relief and comfort for all who are suffering the guilt and shame put upon them in the name of rights. They have been used and they know it. The pro-life camp must enable them to confront and combat their abuser. In doing this it will unleash a force against which the abortionists are helpless. This will prevent other women from making the same mistake.

The Pro-Life Manifesto calls for a ministry of healing that brings these individuals to the loving arms of Christ and to the fellowship of loving and caring people. They are being told that their grief is illegitimate, but we must show them that not only is their grief legitimate, but a healthy sign that they are on the road to recovery from the destructive path that their life has followed ever since they listened to those voices that told them that the road of abortion was the road to greater freedom. They know that it led to imprisonment. They know, too late, that it was a lie. Their need is a need to grieve, and in that grief to receive compassionate help. This help can be richly supplied by those who truly are concerned with their well-being. Remember, the pro-abortionist camp will remain vehemently opposed to such strategy and will claim that we are imposing guilt upon them. That is a natural reaction that can be best overcome by increasing our efforts. As more and more individuals come forth and testify as to the damaging effects abortion has had, cracks will begin to appear in the abortionists' foundation. Many who are now their allies will abandon the abortion rights issue because the evidence against it is too overwhelming. As the crack in the unified dam widens there will be released a force that will cause abortion itself as a desired option to crumble into rubble. Abortion will become odious to women. It will at last be seen to be the demon that it is. There will never be a law that will be as effective as that against abortion, for we will change hearts not laws!

The Pro-Life Manifesto will not only free women, but it will reach out to the vast army of fathers, grandparents, and concerned individuals who genuinely grieve over the tragic loss of life in our midst. Lives will be set free from the hell that now surrounds them. When Christ sets them free, they will be free indeed. No one who has experienced the freedom and peace of the Gospel will ever want to return to the hell of guilt and anguish such as abortion imposes upon its victims. To those in the pro-life camp who do not understand this and feel that the issue must remain free from religion, you are mistaken. Without Christ we cannot offer the suffering anything all that different than the abortionists. They too will be loving and comforting, but they can't offer the peace and joy of sin and guilt washed away. Only Christ can. That is why this portion of the manifesto is so vital. There is no power on earth or in the entire universe as powerful as the love of Christ that sets hearts free. To be effective these victims of abortion must be set free. We simply have no option. We must offer them the hope that they need. To do less would be to insure our failure.

The potential of it is staggering. There are literally millions of men and women who have been damaged by the abortion of their own children. The list of victims goes on and on, and the abortionists daily are adding to that list. They continue to sow the seeds of their own destruction. Up till now that force, though recognized as existing, has not been unleashed as a weapon against abortion. That will have to change. It is our only real hope. If the pro-life forces can come together and make it happen, they will have effectively sent a shock wave across the United States, indeed the world, that will spell doom to the demon that has devoured millions of lives, and with those lives the honor and dignity of an entire people.

Your help is needed to make it happen. The remainder of this book will talk about the important ingredients that will make the manifesto work. There will be a chapter on you and your local church and/or pro-life organization and what it must do to make it all happen. The time to act is now. If your local pro-life group will not act, then start one that will. This issue is too vital to die. The strategy will win, but it needs you and your efforts to succeed. There are many shattered lives depending upon you; please don't let them down.

I ask you to pray that the leadership in the pro-life movement will realize the tremendous potential here. We are a movement together, and the cause of protecting innocent human life has many blessings as well as headaches. I pray that you and your organization are not one of the headaches. We have tried many other approaches, and they have failed. We have seen enough division within the pro-life camp, and we need unity. This is the time. Please get on board, and let's begin an effort that simply won't fail. We can do it, and by God's grace, we will.

SEVEN

Anatomy
of a Victim

In the struggle to free women from the oppression that assails them we must understand that they are under a very heavy burden. That burden is made even heavier by both the pro-life and pro-abortion camps. The pro-life camp is pointing out to her that which she wishes to deny—the fact that she has murdered her baby. The pro-abortion camp is telling her she didn't do anything wrong. Deep inside she realizes that she has to face the truth, but it is difficult to accept facts that tell you that you have caused the death of your child.

Denial and suppression are two natural weapons that a woman employs in dealing with a reality she has difficulty facing. Confusion sets in and she is beset with deep emotional scars leaving her very vulnerable to tremendously powerful forces that are attempting to drive her further and further from ever facing the reality that she must face if things are ever to get better. This condition intensifies when the woman is told by the pro-abortion camp that her grief, guilt, and suffering are not justified, but caused by the actions of the pro-life do-gooders. Instead of relieving her guilt, this has the effect of making that guilt even greater. Now, as confusion sets in, she continues to receive a multitude of contradictory signals that send her on a journey to escape reality. The result is drug addiction, alcohol abuse, suicide, nervous breakdown, or a multitude of emotional and physical symptoms that are screaming to her that something is wrong, very wrong. Her life no longer functions smoothly, and she may not have the vaguest notion as to why.

What is equally important to understand is that for most women, this is completely buried. A woman won't discuss it because she is ashamed of what she has done. She doesn't discuss it because to admit there are problems is to admit that she made a mistake. To admit she made a mistake is to admit that she killed her baby. Deep inside she realizes that she is grieving over the loss of her child, but she cannot come to share that grief with anyone because of the shame that she struggles with. She grasps at psychological crutches to help her deal with a reality she can't accept.

These psychological crutches may manifest themselves in physical ways. In her heart she has already acknowledged that she has murdered her own child. Her fear is that no one will be able to accept that confession lovingly and compassionately. In frightful truth, she is correct. The pro-abortion camp doesn't understand this thinking, for much the same reasons she can't. To admit that abortion causes deep emotional problems would mean to admit they were wrong. To admit this would be chaos. It is much easier to blame the pro-life side for causing the difficulties.

In her heart she knows it is wrong to blame her grief on the pro-life camp, though her mind may desperately grasp for this false hope. The denial that is heaped upon her by her sisters drives her deeper and deeper within herself, for she must not let on to them how disappointed she is with her decision and how terribly hard it is for her to live with it. She already is having a hard time accepting herself, and rejection by her peers would be a devastating blow. She is confronted by a large group of witnesses that are saying that abortion is good and right. These may include family members, clergy, counselors, husband, girlfriends, parents, lover, and women's rights activists. In the face of all of these she is desperate for someone who truly understands the difficulties she faces. She cannot pour her heart out to them, for they are the ones who pressured her into her bad decision or are attempting to reinforce that decision. But she needs to be released, not forced deeper into bondage. She feels that she alone must bear the guilt and burden that has beset her.

If this sounds like an extreme case, let me assure you that it isn't. I know that there are literally millions of women who are facing just such conditions right now. Even more tragically, they have no place to go for help. Some, and it is impossible to say how many, don't make the connection to what is happening in their life and the abortion they have had. Everything is going wrong, slowly but surely wrong, and they don't know why. The reason is buried deep inside, and it is slowly releasing poison throughout their systems and threatens their destruction.

The pro-life camp is adding fuel of another kind to the flames which creates more guilt. They are showing women what they have killed—their babies. The lies that women have chosen to believe come crashing down, and they desperately try to tune those voices out. In protective denial a woman scoffs at the evidence. She turns bitterly against those who wish to help her. They have no idea how to do it. Their intentions are well meant, but their methods are self-defeating. Thus, she is driven deeper within herself, and each step she takes makes it more and more difficult for her to be reached and healed. She takes, unconsciously, escape routes that lead to further destruction.

Ambivalence, mutually conflicting feelings, and confusion develop more and more intensely. "I killed my baby; no, it was a blob of cells and nothing more. I took the coward's way out; no, it was my right, I exercised my right!"

"Why did I kill my baby! Why shouldn't I have the right to do with my body as I choose!"

"It was a child, a baby! No, it wasn't, it wasn't a baby, just cells!"

"Why am I miserable, I hate myself! I want to be loved, I want to love myself. I want others to love me, but who will love me if they know what I did?"

Conflict after conflict piles upon her shoulders, and her condition deteriorates. As anger and bitterness develop, her ability to function properly begins to falter. At first it is hardly noticeable, but the erosion continues and scar tissue develops. Her life takes on changes that she does not understand. Some are internal devices to protect her from the truth. Some are internal devices to punish her. In many instances the carefree life that she sought to gain through the death of her child is slowly lost. Suicide often becomes the last resort to find both peace and punishment.

The conditions and the circumstances vary, but the fact is that abortion causes problems, and these problems are not being dealt with very well. Usually it is the symptom that is treated and not the cause. Symptoms are exactly what they are, and often the counselor a woman turns to is either unaware of the connection between her abortion and what she is suffering, or is pro-abortion and refuses to make the connection. Often it is difficult to make, for the abortion may have occured five to ten years earlier and all seemed well at the time. In fact, if you asked the woman how she felt about her abortion, she might surprise you by saying that it was a great decision on her part. Because it seemed well, the effects of the abortion are accepted as being healthy. This makes it very difficult to connect damaging behavior now being experienced with something that was viewed as good and acceptable so many years earlier. In many instances she never admits she had an abortion. She just buries it.

If this all sounds inconceivable, let me assure you that this is exactly what is happening in real-life situations thousands of times daily. Abortion and its consequences are being buried by women who deny the whole thing, by counselors who cannot or will not make the connection, by parents who don't want to hear about it, by society that doesn't want to be bothered, by woman's rights groups who don't see anything wrong, by pro-life groups who keep up the constant pressure, by fathers who don't want to get involved—the list goes on and on. Meanwhile, the aborted woman bears the brunt alone. She, terribly alone and afraid, doesn't know how to deal with it any better than anyone else. But for her the problem will not go away. She *must* deal with it one way or another, for she has no other choice. The result is that usually she deals with it in ways that are harmful to her psychologically, spiritually, and physically.

To compound the problem, a new and very dangerous development is beginning to happen. Those who run the abortion industry are beginning to cash in even more by establishing counseling centers for their victims. That is comparable to the Nazi Party counseling Jews! Most of the industry is content with using the woman and discarding her baby. They collect their fee and select the next victim. Sometimes an extra sum is collected for patching up a botched job. Usually, however, the woman is tersely told to see her family doctor, and the abortionist hopes that the difficulties she is experiencing can't be linked to a botched abortion. Psychological problems are more easily dismissed, but physical problems get a bit sticky.

It is very difficult to comprehend how many women are suffering irreparable damage because they have been told that their guilt, anxiety, and other problems have nothing to do with their abortion. If they try to connect their suffering to their abortion, they are loaded down with even more guilt because they are told by the pro-abortionists that they should be eternally grateful for their abortions. As the abortionists move into the counseling arena they will in truth be creating a multi-billion dollar industry. That alone is cause for deep alarm, but they will also be creating new problems that will drive women into deeper and deeper despair from which it will be virtually impossible to emerge. Essentially, the abortionists will be able to compound their culpability and in the process get paid for it. The women will be victimized again.

The woman who has undergone an abortion needs help, real, emphathetic help. She does not need someone to trivialize her grief. She does not need further and more damaging lies. She needs to grieve and to do so in a setting that allows freedom to grieve without the added burden of further guilt. If she had lost an infant to disease, accident, or miscarriage, society would be very understanding of her grief and give her needed support in it. There are all kinds of support systems for a woman facing that type of grief. When she has aborted her child, there is no sympathetic voice to calm her. The group that persuaded her to kill her child doesn't want to hear her grief—that is simply not acceptable behavior. She is told she is weak and being manipulated by the pro-lifers or that her feelings are wrong. When she was someone they could make a buck off of or a pawn in their ideology, the abortionists supported her. Now, when her usefulness to them is over, she is an embarrassment, a disgrace. Furthermore, she threatens the feminist assertion that no one suffers from abortions. Therefore, she is rejected. It is not difficult to imagine the mess that those of the pro-abortion persuasion will make of her life if they also begin the counseling procedure. I am sure that they will milk the situation for all it's worth and then discard her when they have gotten all that they can out of her. This is a terrible and sad situation, and it's happening now.

Except for groups like WEBA, at this time the pro-life side has precious little to offer in this area. There simply is noplace for a woman to go. Her pastor may either not understand or not be pro-life. If he is pro-life, but legalistic, she may suffer as surely at his hands as at the hands of the pro-abortionists. Every direction she turns seems to be blocked. She needs help, she needs understanding and forgiveness and she needs it now. It is not often that she finds it.

The Pro-Life Manifesto requires that we begin to destroy abortion from within. To do that we must begin to release women who are suffering from the bondage that has seized them. We must first help them regain their composure and nurture them in the love of Christ. Until we have done that, they won't be very effective in the fight to end abortion. To be able to provide for their needs will require more than just an organization dedicated to helping them. It will take a well-equipped organization that has something special to offer and which will allow women to muster the courage to come out into the open and seek and receive the help they need. That something special is the love and forgiveness of Christ compassionately ministered by those who have been there.

WEBA is part of the key. If the proper atmosphere is created, I am convinced that the results will be absolutely shocking. Women will start coming out as neither side ever dreamed. There will be a revolution within our country, and the first victim will be abortion. The reason is obvious. If you have several million women openly accusing the abortion industry of destroying their life and describing the hell that they have been going through, people are going to start to listen. When we become aware of the extent of this national tragedy, we will not have to worry about electing enough pro-life congressmen. Those already serving will join the bandwagon and abortion will die.

It will be a movement that abortionists can't stop because of the very nature of what abortion is and does. The abortionists may deny what I am saying, but let me assure you that they fear this type of an attack more than thousands of picketers or brochures or attempts to elect pro-life politicians. There will be nothing more devastating to them than an army of angry women, their victims, demanding truth and justice. As for the leaders of the women's rights movement, how will they explain why they sold these women down the drain? How will they explain why they weren't more interested in their welfare? How will they justify promoting something that destroyed so many so cruelly as abortion did? The women's rights groups will have but one choice—denounce abortion and say they were deceived. The axe will eventually fall where it must, on the neck of the abortionist.

Let me say a word to the women and men who are currently leading the fight to preserve abortion rights. You are going to have to eat crow, and I can't wait to watch. In saying that I don't mean to make light of the subject, but it's the same feeling you get when the villain in a movie finally gets what he's got coming. He walked all over the innocent and finally he has to face the music. I can hear their sick, whining voices as they attempt to excuse themselves from the guilt they bear.

"Oh, we weren't really for abortion. We were forced into it because there wasn't any other solution." Well, ladies and gentlemen, no one will buy it. We are on to you, and we will watch you fall. In your place will arise a new generation of leadership that will not manipulate women but serve them. That will be a glorious day for our country, and it's a day that is coming soon!

If we of the pro-life camp follow the correct strategy and not get sidetracked, we will see that day. Victory is not that far away, but we have much work to do and it must begin now.

EIGHT

A Place
for Healing

Whenever someone is suffering emotional wounds, they need a place to go where they can be alone and work things out. It may be their room, or a study, or the solitude of the shore, car, woods, or church. What is needed is a place where they can reflect, and through prayer and meditation be renewed and strengthened. When we lose someone very dear to us we often go to their grave site and grieve for them there. We find comfort and healing in being able to go to where we feel closer to that loved one who is not with us. There is a need for that physical burial place, for some evidence of their having existed, because it helps us recover from our loss and deal with death. For people who lose a loved one whose body is not recovered, there is often more difficulty in accepting their death. We need to bury our dead. Burial helps put to rest feelings that arise deep within us that we may not fully understand.

Many women who have had an abortion are attempting to deal with deep feelings when they place a grave marker at a family plot, or purchase a plot in a cemetery and put a marker there for their lost baby. There is an emptiness that they are trying to fill, and that void is made more difficult because there are no remains to grieve over. Their baby is gone and they know not where. There is a void that cannot be filled, and their attempts to fill it are often pathetic and extremely sad. Their babies are missing, and they don't know what to do.

If that sounds abnormal to you, let me assure you that it is not. It is a healthy way to deal with a real and devastating tragedy that has overpowered an aborted woman. Her baby, her unwanted baby, is gone and she wishes she could have it back, for now she realizes the foolishness of her actions. She wants it back, but there is no way to bring it back. The child is gone, forever, and it is gone because, as she begins to see, she was selfish and was looking out only for herself. I can't imagine how horrible that must be for her to accept. She must be burdened with a load of guilt and sorrow that comes to the point of breaking her spirit. For her, there is noplace to go, no refuge, no burial ground. Normally, with the loss of a child she would receive all kinds of support, but she must bear all of this alone, for there is no one she can really turn to that she can trust to understand.

There really is noplace for her. The church to which she belongs, if she belongs to one, may or may not provide for her needs. Most likely it can't, for few pastors are equipped to deal with her grief. Actually a pastor should be able to, but too often he doesn't. She is alone and afraid. Sometimes it is that fear that will restrain her from seeking help. Fear and shame are powerful enemies standing in her path to recovery. Her self-esteem is at an all-time low. In fact, it has dropped dangerously to where she is ready to attempt any means of escape from the hell that is going on inside her. This is a sad, frightening picture of what millions of women are experiencing because of abortion. Why don't we hear more about them? Because they are afraid, and in that fear they have buried their feelings. Because we don't want to understand. There is a harsh old saying: she made her bed, let her sleep in it. Part of it is apathy. People just don't care if it doesn't affect them directly. Certainly part of its arises out of the fact that she made a deliberate decision, and we expect her to have the guts to stand behind that decision. We have to remember, that decision was made on the basis of lies.

There is a project that holds much hope and promise for the woman in this position, and it is the National Memorial to the Unborn Child. The name of it is a bit misleading, for it is more than a memorial. It is a Mourning Center for women who have had an abortion. It is a place where they can identify their baby as belonging. They can go there and know that this is dedicated to their child. It is dedicated to them and to all who grieve the loss of innocent life in our midst. There is only one problem—the Memorial hasn't been built yet.

We need this project now! It is part of the key to ending abortion in America. I am fully convinced of that fact or I wouldn't be backing the project so extensively. Actually, the project is much more complicated than just erecting a memorial. It involves saving lives through a very well planned system. The National Memorial project is actually two distinct yet very related systems. The first is the Memorial itself. Later I will describe it in detail and how each part will fill a needed role in the Pro-Life Manifesto. It is a healing facility. As a healing facility, it will serve a purpose far beyond any tool available today. It will be located either in Washington, D.C., or St. Louis. The Washington site is desired because it is the site of so many memorials. The St. Louis site is desired because it is geographically centered. Around the country Mourning Centers must be established. These will be places where women can go to grieve and to receive supportive counseling. They will be patterned after the main Memorial's chapel. There needs to be a Mourning Center in easy reach of all regions of the country. I envision over one hundred of these spread throughout the land.

The Mourning Center is a serene structure which is designed to provide a quiet, peaceful setting for a woman or man to come and mourn for the babies lost to abortion. In most instances it will be for a specific child. It provides an outlet for that grief and at the same time provides a stationary, permanent place that the person can identify as being the place dedicated to a specific child. It is a strong statement to the grieving person that there are people who care and who will help.

Several important things are meant to happen at the Mourning Center. First, there is a time for prayer and meditation. This is a purifying process which enables the woman to express her loss and to pray for forgiveness and healing. The chapel is made personal for her through the use of signature tiles that enable her to dedicate her child very specifically. Many people do not realize that many women have named their aborted baby. The death date, or birth date—actually the due date—are very important dates to her. The chapel wall will be lined with a very personal touch that will bring the reality of the abortion tragedy home to anyone who visits. When a woman needs to grieve she can take great comfort in the fact that here, at the chapel, is the grave marker for her child. If we provide these grieving places they will be used, and there will be healing and forgiveness such as we never realized a need for before. The Mourning Centers are a must! We need them to make the Pro-Life Manifesto work.

What I am about to say will upset some of you very greatly, but it is true nevertheless, and you need to understand this truth if you will ever understand the way that healing and strength will come to those who suffer because of abortion. There is no healing without the forgiveness offered through Jesus Christ. When God sent His Son into the world it was to atone for the sins of the world. Jesus gave his lifeblood at Calvary, and with that sacrifice a sinner can find peace and hope. The God of creation, who gave the woman her child in the first place, can also give her peace through the blood of Jesus Christ. We have an individual who is loaded down with grief and sorrow. She knows she killed her child, and she knows that she needs to make peace with God, her child, and herself. She needs to have her burden lifted and the knowledge that through Jesus Christ her sins are forgiven. It is only when she has made peace with God that she can begin to make peace with herself and with the world that allowed such a horrible thing to happen to her.

In the Book of Acts 13:32-39 the Apostle Paul is addressing the people and he speaks these words to them:

> And we declare to you glad tidings, how that the promise which was made unto the fathers, God has fulfilled the same unto us their children, in that he raised up Jesus again; as it is also written in the second Psalm, "Thou art my Son, this day I have begotten thee." And as concerning that he raised him up from the dead, now no more to return to corruption, he said on this wise, "I will give you the sure mercies of David." Wherefore he saith also in another Psalm, "Thou shalt not suffer thine Holy One to see corruption." For David, after he fell asleep, was laid unto his fathers, and saw corruption: but he, whom God raised again, saw no corruption. Be it known to you brethren, that through this man is preached unto you the forgiveness of sins: and by him all that believe are justified from all things, from which ye could not be justified by the law of Moses.

If we attempt to provide healing to those who suffer because of abortion and do not do so through the forgiveness of Jesus, we are making a very serious mistake. Christ came that whoever believes on Him should not perish but have everlasting life. The woman knows that she has violated God's law, and that by that law she deserves death and judgment. The law can only drive her deeper and deeper into despair. To ignore her act against the Creator God is to deny what she knows to be true. That denial will lead her not to trust but be suspicious of counsel given her. Far worse, it will leave her in her sins! If we are to help her, we have to help her get free from her sins. She is already burdened with guilt. It is this burden of guilt that has her weighed down, and that weight must be relieved. It does absolutely more harm than good to tell her that she has nothing to feel guilty about or that God understands and that she doesn't need to repent, only understand herself.

Some try to remove God from the picture altogether, and that is a deadly mistake. We must not bow to the Satanic pressure that this must not be a religious issue. When we bring a person to the healing forgiveness of Jesus we are not bringing them to religion. We are not talking about a dead system of "do's" and "don'ts"; we are talking about a risen Lord! We are talking about one who demonstrated once and for all that death has no hold over Him or over those who believe in His name! Unless we bring a woman to the very forgiveness of Jesus, we leave her in despair and have not done anything for her worth doing.

Christ is the stumbling block: the stone which the builders rejected. That's what the Apostle Peter stated in 1 Peter 2:1-8:

> Therefore, rid yourselves of all malice, and all deceit, hypocrisy, envy and slander of every kind. Like newborn babies, crave pure spiritual milk, so that by it you may grow up in your salvation; now that you have tasted that the Lord is good. As you come to Him, the living stone—rejected by men but chosen by God and precious to Him—you also, like the living stones, are being built into a spiritual house to be a holy priesthood, offering spiritual sacrifices acceptable to God through Jesus Christ. For in Scripture it says: "See I lay a stone in Zion, a chosen and precious cornerstone and the one who trusts in Him will never be put to shame." Now to you who believe, this stone is precious. But to those who do not believe, "The stone the builders rejected has become the cornerstone" and "A stone that causes men to stumble and a rock that makes them fall."

Therein is the truth of our situation: unless we bring Christ into the picture we have virtually nothing to offer. We are dealing with guilt-laden women who have acted in a manner that has left them rejected and in despair. While we can temporarily fool her into believing that everything is all right because we say it is, we are only doing for her what got her into all of the trouble in the first place. She was told that it was all right to have an abortion. She was told that it would do her no harm. She was told that she would be able to have a normal, peace-filled life once the burden of an unwanted pregnancy was over. She was told a blatant lie, and now she knows it was a lie, but it's too late. To attempt to appease her guilt-filled conscience by trying to tell her that although she made a mistake she can forgive herself and go on will do nothing but leave her with her guilt. She may also feel a great deal of anger for the pro-life side that did not offer her any more than the abortionist side did. We must take her to a higher power, one which can relieve her of her terrible guilt and give her peace. There is only one such power, and that is the living Lord Jesus Christ.

Some may say that if we present Jesus Christ as the only answer, we risk being accused of imposing our morality upon someone else. That position is worthless and we must come to recognize it and label it as such. Abortion is forcing its twisted morality upon our nation and is leading us down a path of destruction. The feminists have used lies and deceptive tactics to impose their will upon society. We have something "chosen and precious" to offer, and we had better realize that fact and not be ashamed of it. If we are ashamed of Jesus, then we too are falling over the stone which the builders rejected. If there are those in the pro-life movement who do not wish to put forth Christ, so be it, but they don't have much to offer.

There is no salvation in any other name. I realize that the feminists are going to have a field day with that statement, but let me say it again; there is salvation in no other name. If we are to win the battle for life, we had better begin to realize that we need to offer hope and healing. In hope and healing we will be raising up an army of once-defeated and desperate individuals who have come to a love that knows no bounds. If they had known that love before their abortion, they would not have experienced the emptiness and anguish that they went through. They would also have their baby, alive.

We are not in the business of trying to please men. We are here to do the service of God. When a woman comes to us and needs the healing and forgiveness of Christ and we offer her something else, we are giving her a stone instead of bread. That is where WEBA comes back into the picture. These women have come to the fountain of living water and drank deeply. They have found the healing that comes through Christ. They are born again. Their life has been released from the bondage that abortion put it in, and they can now serve the living God with their life. They now have something to offer other women who are where they were. They can smile again, and they know that God has forgiven them. With that knowledge they can learn to forgive themselves. That is healing! That's what makes the Savior's love so precious! He brings ruined souls something the world cannot offer—peace, and with peace, life.

The Memorial will be a place where women can be counseled not only in the peace that comes through grieving, but also in the Lord Jesus Christ. He is the power that will set them free. Once He has, they will never be in bondage again. The women of WEBA have impressed me more than any other group of women. They suffered under a heavy load, they went through hell, but they have a Savior and they found peace within their soul. They are strong and determined, for they are resolved to end abortion. They know abortion for what it is, a cold deadly killer. They know what horror it put them through, and they are determined to expose it. They know, because they heard and believed the lies put forth to induce women to kill their babies. They are an extremely important part of the effort to end abortion. The Mourning Centers and the National Memorial to the Unborn Child is for them and women like them. It is for everyone who needs to grieve and remember those who died for no other crime than that they weren't wanted.

Lorijo Nerad, International President of WEBA, wrote these words about the Memorial:

The grieving mothers and fathers of our country will have an added touch of healing in their lives when the National Memorial to the Unborn Child is built. Others, whose life has been shattered by the untimely death of their unborn grandchild, sibling, nephew, or niece, will find in the Memorial a source of healing also. The Memorial is for both the living and the lost.

We have been known to build statues and memorials to pay tribute to our dead. The soldiers who have fought for freedom, men and women who have given their lives to society, have been recognized for their deeds. Millions of unborn children, who had died through abortion, have lost their lives in a war waged against the family. They were defenseless victims of a cruel enemy, abortion, before they ever had a chance to make a contribution to society. We shall never know what contribution some of them might have made to our society.

We need the Memorial to the Unborn Child to symbolically bury our dead. We need it to open the eyes of those who have aborted their children, to start the healing process, and to add healing to those who now realize what they have done. The Pool of Tears will have many tears of forgiveness, and years of guilt will be released. Some have carried burdens of grief for years. They need the Memorial to finalize their loss. The chapel will be a place where they can come to quietly seek God's peace.

Women Exploited By Abortion is honored to be a part of the National Memorial to the Unborn Child. Our calling is to minister to the brokenhearted, to set the captive free through Jesus Christ. He can work through the Memorial, and many can be set free.

Please help us see this healing come to pass and help us help the National Memorial to the Unborn Child become a reality.

The women of WEBA wept tears when they saw the scale model of the Memorial. You see, they understand what those who have not gone through the hell they have can't grasp. The Memorial will bring healing to so many by bringing them to the loving arms of Jesus Christ. It will be their special place to pray and mourn, and it will be much more. We will spend a chapter on the Memorial, for it is a vital part of all that we are attempting to accomplish. We will also spend a chapter on the Mourning Centers, for they are the right arm of the Memorial. These are the tools of the manifesto. These are not options, they are necessities. We need them now, and we need them desperately.

NINE

The Mourning Centers

What has been most difficult is to convince the different pro-life groups that the strategy they are using is not effectively fighting abortion. In many ways there seems to be a more urgent concern to propagate an organization than to devise an effective strategy to end this deadly killer. Probably one of the major reasons for this is that whenever you have a struggle such as this occurring, each faction believes that it is doing the proper thing and as a result is reluctant to give itself over to outsiders and their ideas.

Amazing as it may seem, WEBA has not gotten the overwhelming support that it should be getting. Too many pro-life groups have not had the vision to realize the damage that this organization can do to the pro-abortion cause. Others, who do realize the effectiveness of such a group of women, have tried to remove Christ from the picture. What they have done is attempt to take a group of hurting women and offer them exactly what the world is offering them— comfort without healing. That simply cannot be done. To attempt to do that is to attempt to rectify a horrible situation without the main ingredient to rectification. These women are deeply hurt and suffering. No counselor can give them the peace and hope that our Lord Jesus Christ can. When they have sinned against God and all that is in His law, they cannot be restored by supportive counseling alone.

They cannot be given power to become strong allies in the struggle to end abortion. They can only be made better by receiving the freeing, saving, empowering forgiveness of Jesus Christ. Without that, they will remain ineffective.

We must develop a strategy that not only draws these women out into the open, but also gives them the strength and courage to face the oppressor. Believe me, the abortionist camp knows how to exploit their weakness, and they do it ruthlessly. Instead of calling them to healing and helping them deal with the inner turmoil, they call their grief and suffering a product of misguided individuals in society that are pushing that guilt upon them. They tell them to be strong and resist those who are trying to convince them that they have done something wrong. They tell them, by reinforcement, that they made a wise decision and that they should now live with it. This method is no more effective than pro-life attempts to help women without Christ. It may help for a little while, but it won't sustain them in the long run. Time does not ease the guilt and suffering; it is always there and often the slightest thing can awaken great degrees of guilt and anxiety.

A woman suffering because of her abortion needs to be forgiven by God, and that can only be done by the blood of Jesus. If we fail to take her to the cross, we have failed to really help her, and her life will reflect that failure. Christ can set her free. As His child she can learn to smile and laugh again, and to do it free from the burden she has felt all these years.

If there is a legitimate gripe against the pro-life forces, it is that they have contributed to aborted women's grief without providing a clear and correct way to alleviate it. Too few groups are offering the suffering woman the only real answer to her grief—the forgiveness, healing, and restoration that come from Jesus Christ. The woman, too often, has no one to turn to, and she adds loneliness to an already serious situation. If the pro-life forces are serious about ending abortion, and I believe they are, they must also become serious about healing the woman's scars due to her abortion. They must find ways to help these women become a strong and effective force in preventing other women from making the same mistake. That can be accomplished, but it will take an effective strategy and much cooperation. Otherwise we will condemn the pro-life movement to a merry-go-round existence. We are moving, but in circles. We are excited because things seem to be progressing, but in truth they are going nowhere.

What we need is a tool, a strong, effective tool, to bring shy and fearful women into the open. A tool that will speak to them about the healing that they can have. A tool that will enable and equip an army of women to combat this destructive, demonic evil that has beset us. These next two chapters are meant to design such a tool, explain how it works, and show how it can be most effectively used.

As I have stated, the National Memorial to the Unborn Child is more than some brick and mortar erected to the memory of millions of babies who were killed by abortion. It is a means of helping women who are suffering from the effects of an abortion. Those effects were addressed previously, but it is important to remember that they are very real and much more debilitating than we like to admit. The woman who has had an abortion faces a very lonely existence. She is filled with grief and remorse and does not know where to turn. Because she has so much anxiety and guilt, she is afraid that she will be exposed to even greater condemnation if she reveals her plight. Often, when she does choose to reveal the struggle that she is experiencing, it is to someone in the pro-abortion camp. One would think that these individuals would give her a great deal of support and that they would help her through her crisis.

The result is usually quite different. The pro-abortionists are not equipped to handle the problems that the abortion process is creating. How could they? With their ideological commitment to abortion, they simply don't dare admit that it is destroying the lives of the women who have selected that method of dealing with their pregnancy. The pro-abortionists have invested too much emotional and intellectual stock into abortion to admit it is wrong.

Having destroyed the woman's baby through the abortion process, they are now, and I am sure without realizing it, destroying her. The abortion has already damaged her greatly. Now, through its devastating effects, they are doing even greater damage. These are not vicious, criminal people who are purposely destroying women. But they have created a monster, a monster that is effectively destroying millions upon millions of lives. It will take a real shock to get them to see the truth of the matter. Some of them will never see it.

The shock that will affect the women's rights movement, society at large, and even the pro-life camp is going to arise from the suffering men and women who are the victims of abortion. In short, the living victims will be the strongest force to combat this deadly killer. To do this we must provide a safe vehicle for them that will allow them to express their grief and come to the healing which they so desperately need. That is where the National Memorial and the Mourning Centers come in.

When I first presented the Memorial project it was a failure. That's because I failed to share the true vision of what the Memorial project meant for the people who could best be helped by it, and for the people who could best help it. While I was seeing a positive, excited, and deeply moving reaction of the woman who had had an abortion, that same response was often missing from the larger segment of the pro-life community.

What I usually got were responses which reflected a "that's nice, but . . ." posture. "That's nice, but we need to get more political influence first." "That's nice, but we need to educate people first." "That's nice, but why spend so much money on brick and mortar?" "That's nice, but why not wait until after the battle is won and abortion is banned?"

The "that's nice, but . . ." responses went on and on until I could almost predict answers before they were stated.

It all depended upon which camp the person was most influenced by. The failure was mine, for I failed to realize that others didn't have the same vision that I did. Oh, WEBA and women who have suffered an abortion almost always did, but only a handful of others. Those that did gave me a different "that's nice, but . . ." response. It was, "That's nice, but we don't have the time to help. We have our own projects to worry about."

The women who suffer have no problem in seeing what it will do for them and women like them. I assumed that if they could, then certainly everyone else in the pro-life camp would as well. I was wrong! I have since discovered that the pro-life people are as in the dark about the consequences of abortion as the abortionists are. The big difference is that they will listen, whereas the other side won't. They simply have not comprehended that abortion is destroying women. They are open and warm to such women, for the most part, and assume that these women will be free and open with them. They don't understand the fear and guilt that these women are under. It is these two forces, fear and guilt, that are preventing them from coming out into the open for healing. The pro-life camp merely wants them to admit they made a mistake and believes that when they have made that admission they will soon be all better.

It just doesn't work that way! The pro-life camp thinks that because they accept a woman and forgive her for what she has done, that she is in the clear, that her experience is all over with. While she needs acceptance and forgiveness from others, she also needs to be rid of her fear and guilt. She is mourning the death of her child, and she finds herself in a self-imposed hell. She needs to be set free, and that freedom can only come from Jesus Christ.

There is where the pro-life camp has failed miserably, for it has failed to offer her a safe and acceptable route to receive healing. In most cases it has failed to offer Christ's love at all. In other instances it has no safe vehicle to do so. That is the key to understanding the meaning of the Mourning Centers and the Memorial! Until there is a safe vehicle which can bring suffering women to the healing that they need, most of them will never seek that healing at all. If they do, if will be from the wrong source. It will be from the abortionist camp. That, without doubt, will be disaster.

What we need to establish, and we must do it at a fast pace, are Mourning Centers. A Mourning Center is a place of refuge for a woman where she can come and mourn and deal with her loss, with her fear, and with her guilt. It is a place where her dead child is commemorated. It has to be specifically dedicated to this cause, and its design must be with this purpose in mind.

The Mourning Center is crucial in the process of healing aborted women. It is a place where the loss of innocent children and the forgiveness offered in Jesus Christ come together. The local church cannot do this for several reasons, but primarily because it is not identified directly with helping abortion victims. It represents a threat to hurting women who understandably fear many elements in society, among them the church. Part of the difficulty lies with the clergy who have not taken open and compassionate stands against this evil. Part of it lies in the very nature of the church itself. Most of these women are not active in a church, especially one that proclaims the true Gospel. They see the church as a threat, for they fear its condemnation. Some have turned to churches, especially pro-abortion churches, and have not received any more than if they had gone to the abortionists. That is to the church's shame.

Women who are non-Christians don't see the church as a place to turn to, nor do they see any connection between the agony they suffer and what the church can offer. Notice, the church is not always creating the problem. Certainly confusion over who or what the church is does create problems, for it makes identification of a source of hope almost impossible. No matter how compassionate a particular church may be, most suffering women will not be able to sufficiently overcome their fear to trust it. For an aborted woman, the church may create negative feelings of fear and suspicion.

It is also important to remember that both Christians and non-Christians are suffering. The Mourning Center is established for a woman and her lost child. She knows that, and she knows that there will be help there. She knows where to turn. Let that sink in deep: she knows where to turn. There will be help there. She knows that this center is her place to turn.

The Mourning Center is set up as follows: A chapel, a memorial, an identification coupler, an education center, and a counseling center.

The Mourning Center is fashioned in many ways to be a link to the main Memorial. Thus, in the Mourning Center there will be a miniature Pool of Tears. The Pool of Tears is a black, cylindrical marble pillar that has a shallow pool atop it. Every twenty seconds, or the rate of death due to abortion, a drop of water will fall into the pool. The pool will be of a much smaller scale than the National Memorial's pool. In the main Memorial the pool is also located in a symbolic location. This will be discussed in more detail in the next chapter. It is a simple but powerful reminder that there are tears being shed for and by each child that is killed. It is a symbol of mourning. The connecting link between the Mourning Center and the National Memorial is important. This helps a woman to make a positive identification between her child and a beautiful place to rest. The picture that many women have is of their baby in a garbage can, an incinerator, a laboratory, in cosmetics, or in a whole host of other real or imaginary places. The Memorial helps women to think of their babies as being in a safe place. That alone helps her to ease her guilt.

A woman needs to regard this Mourning Center as her own special place. The center must become personal to her and her child. The walls of the chapel are lined with signature tiles. The signature tile is the direct link which "buries" her child at this location. Many women who have aborted a child have also named that child, and the tiles can be made as personal as a woman wishes. The important thing is that she is able to identify this place as the place to come and mourn her baby. That enables her to deal with her sin, fear, and guilt. The tile says in her heart, "My child is here. My child received a decent burial. I know where my child is, and I can come here and mourn." With that thought there is a measure of peace. It is a first and important step toward healing.

It is hard to imagine a chapel with its walls being directly connected to those unknown, yet dearly missed babies who never had a chance to live beyond their mother's womb. These tiles are the identification link. The impact of this will be very humbling and emotional. The impact upon those who grieve will be enormous, and very vital. It will be a vehicle that will help set them free. It will be a vital link between a woman and her baby. But this is only the beginning. There are two other important areas, the education center and the counseling center.

The education center is not primarily designed to educate the public about the child in the womb. Its main purpose is to help the grieving woman understand herself and her emotions better. It is also designed to help those who have not had an abortion understand those who have. Thus, it is designed to help facilitate understanding of both the child and the mother. This is a very non-threatening form of therapy. A woman can gain insight into herself and what has been happening that has caused her so much turmoil and confusion. In understanding herself she can begin to see the way to seek even further help—and that is where the counseling center is critical.

The counseling center is vital to the Mourning Center, as it is to the main Memorial. The impact that her abortion has had upon a woman is far beyond what most realize. The abortion also affects fathers, grandparents and a host of others. For some the experience of being able to come to a special place is sufficient, but for others it is not. They will need to be able to pour out their anguish and sorrow before the Lord. As they do the healing will begin. For others the process is much more difficult and painful. They need and should have immediate, compassionate help. They need to be led out of the wilderness of grief, guilt and confusion. They need the compassionate love and forgiveness of Jesus Christ. They need to be assisted in dealing with their grief in a manner that fosters acceptance of their loss and rejection of all of the destructive ways they have been attempting to deal with it in the past.

Why Jesus Christ? Why not keep it open to people of all faiths and backgrounds? Why not allow people of all beliefs to come and receive healing and strength? First, people of all beliefs and backgrounds can and will come. A woman does not need to be a Christian to come to the Mourning Center and grieve over the loss of her child. The Mourning Center will be open to individuals of all faiths and beliefs. The fact is, however, that outside of Jesus Christ, there cannot be true healing and peace.

As women carry their burdens to the Savior, they can be released permanently from all of the heartache and sorrow that surrounds their life. They can be empowered to become a visible and active force to ending abortion. They can be set free from the trap that they have lived with and serve the living God. They can withstand the barrage of conflicts, doubts, and anguish that assail them and rob them of peace. They can deal with the anger that cries out for revenge upon the lives of the butchers who led them to the clinic and stole the lives of their babies.

Jesus Christ performs miracles. He can heal their scars. While they will always remember their aborted children and grieve, they will have a peace that they never had before. They will be given the strength to live life fully again and not have to be tormented by the loss of their child. It is that torment that has resulted in destructive behavior. It is that torment that has led to the complete destruction of many women and will lead to the destruction of many more.

Jesus Christ alone can bring healing. He alone could have taken a woman's aborted child in His arms and shown the love and compassion that was needed to allow the child to live. He alone could have given the women strength and courage to face a future which allowed both mother and child to live. Jesus Christ is the Lord of life and forgiveness. There simply is no one else to turn to. For the soul that suffers in anguish and sorrow, Christ alone can bring sweet peace—a peace that cannot be described, but once tasted, will never be forgotten.

I could go on and on about the need for the Savior. Many will scoff at that need unless they receive Him. Then there will arise in them such hope and life that they will come to know and realize how beautiful life can be. Rachel is truly weeping for her children and she refuses to be comforted, for they are no more, but she can be given hope in the atoning blood of Jesus Christ.

The Mourning Centers will offer some degree of peace. They need to be built in all major population areas of the country. They need to be built now and at a rapid rate. They need to be staffed by WEBA counselors, for they understand and can begin the critical healing process.

TEN

The
National
Memorial

When the idea for the National Memorial to the Unborn Child came to me, I was driving in my car. The idea hit me solidly in my heart. I had been praying for a solution to abortion in America, and I knew that what was being done, while holding ground, was not going to win the battle. We needed something much more dramatic, much more obvious. Something which could not be hidden or denied. The Memorial was an answer to that need, but it was much more than that as well. It was a center for healing for the wounded. Mothers, fathers, grandparents, and countless others could come and receive hope and peace.

Abortion is taking the heart out of our country, and we need to find a way to stop it from progressing any further. We are losing our sensitivity to pain and suffering. Our solutions are now to avoid responsibility even if it means the death of innocent life and the destruction of the life that remains. What I did not perceive at that time was the need for Mourning Centers to go hand and hand with the Memorial. Without the centers the Memorial is not complete. Without the Memorial the centers are not complete. They must work together.

The Memorial can accomplish what education, politics, picketing, and protesting cannot accomplish. It can effectively end abortion by the release of a powerful force that will tear abortion apart from the inside. None of the other methods will do that, for even if we succeed in blocking abortions, we will not have succeeded in clearly and effectively demonstrating that abortion is extremely harmful to the woman who has had one. If we cannot show clearly the damage to aborted women, we will not be able to show the woman who is contemplating one the imminent dangers to herself as well as her child. Most abortions will turn underground, and the pro-life community will cease its relentless efforts, thinking that it has won. The enemy will not have been defeated, only forced to seek different ways to spread their poison. The fight will continue only with the tables turned. What is the point of that? No, we must find a way to convince the liberal forces that abortion is not all that they have thought it to be. Abortion must be an embarrassment for them. That can be done, but it will first take some vision on the part of the pro-life community.

To date few in the pro-life community have had that vision. The Memorial has been labeled by some as a bunch of mortar and brick. If the pro-life community does not come to recognize what the Memorial really means, it is missing a golden opportunity to accomplish what has been only a dream to date—the end of abortion. The sad part is that too many lack such vision to see what the Memorial project can accomplish. They see it as a threat to their own group's finances rather than as a weapon to be fashioned to combat abortion and its proponents. Not all see it that way, but unfortunately too many do. This is not the time for blindness. We need leadership with vision and imagination. It takes courage to attempt something radical and new like this project, but the results will be astounding.

The Memorial will be a wedge within the pro-abortionist camp to cause division and confusion. There will be attacks upon their leadership and questions of honesty and integrity, for it will soon be evident that the leadership of many of the women's activist groups has sold out the pregnant woman and her child for poliical advantage. It is such leadership that should stand trial much like the Nazi war criminals, because they have led millions of innocent victims to a cruel death. They knew what they were doing, and that makes it all the more enraging. If this sounds like a harsh indictment of groups who are leading women, it is. Why? Because it is obvious that they realize the extent of the damage being done far more than they are publicly admitting. They are not blind guides; their eyes are wide open and they see the suffering and pain. They know that babies are being killed and women ruined, but they do it for the cause, their cause. They believe that the end will justify the means, but the means is an unspeakable horror! They are without excuse. Someday they will realize the final outcome of their betrayal. We do not need to judge them; their judgment will be swift and final. God will be that judge.

Currently the pro-life forces are playing right into their hands, and they are being soundly defeated. The pro-life strategy of external pressure is only unifying them and encouraging them to become stronger. We must work powerfully and relentlessly from within, and as we do they will be destroyed.

At this time I will describe the physical layout of the Memorial which includes the following: 1) The Memorial design itself; 2) the Pool of Tears; 3) the Chapel; 4) the Auditorium and Education Center; 5) the Identification Link; 6) the Burial Vault.

The Memorial is designed to be a delicate but beautiful spiral that reaches eighty feet in height. The same delicate spiral, made of white marble, looks entirely different when viewed from the floor-plan drawing. Thus, the two illustrations give two completely different pictures of the Memorial. Figure A is the sketch of the Memorial as looking straight down upon it. Notice the close resemblance to early life in the womb. The Pool of Tears forms the eye of the baby, and that is not without significance. An actual drawing of the scale model would reveal something entirely different. Rather than the awkward lines of the floor plan, we would see the beauty and grace of the actual Memorial.

The Memorial to the Unborn Child reflects the differ-

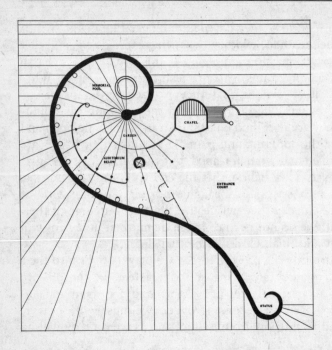

ence between a description and an actuality. Milt Martinson & Associates of Green Bay designed the Memorial, and they did a tremendously sensitive job. We who are for this little child in the womb are in deep gratitude to him and his staff for their excellent design. As he and his associates labored over this project I had asked them to complete, it became apparent that theirs was a labor of love. God was truly guiding their efforts, and the Memorial reflects the beauty and grace that I had hoped for.

The Pool of Tears is the heart of the Memorial. It is highly symbolic. First, the pool itself is twenty feet across and over sixteen feet high. It is made out of black marble. On the sides of the marble will be engraved the names of those individuals who helped to make the Memorial possible. They place their name there in witness that their tears are being shed for the death of so many innocent lives. In Chapter 12 you will find how to have your name included. On the surface of the pool will be a single, symbolic rose.

The rose has become the pro-life symbol, and that symbol will also be evident in the fact that the greenery that makes up the inside of the Memorial will be primarily roses. Every twenty seconds, just like at the Mourning Centers, a single drop of water will hit the surface of the pool. Each drop represents an aborted child. It is a simple yet commanding reminder that the killing is going on in spite of our sorrow, efforts, and desire. Built into the pool will be a counter that keeps a record of each life as it is lost. Every twenty seconds another number . . . another life lost . . . another tiny baby destroyed . . . The death toll goes on, urging our efforts not to cease, pleading with us to double, triple our efforts. And the drops are like a cry from the unborn dead saying please, oh please, don't forget that we were, that we lived, even if for such a brief moment. When, oh, when will it end!

Deep in the recesses of the Memorial, in the solitude of the vaults, will lie some of those whose life was not deemed worthy to allow to live. The Memorial will have its victims, both the living and the dead. It is a shame that so few of the millions of lives can be provided a peaceful resting place. Let the reader take comfort in the fact that the souls of those who have never seen the sun nor felt their mother's touch rest in the peaceful arms of the Savior. There, death is no more and He has wiped every tear from their eyes. There, though they never felt love here on earth, they are loved and cherished. There they are at peace.

In that regard, Lorijo Nerad, International President of WEBA, has designed a statue which depicts a mother reaching up through the clouds to her child, which the Savior has in His arms. She cannot quite reach the child, for it is just beyond her outstretched arms, but the child is safe in the arms of Jesus. She has one foot planted upon earth, and she will have to await the resurrection before she will ever get to hold the child that once was hers. It is a powerful statue, and it will be an important part of the Memorial.

How many women have suffered in this world dreaming of the day when they will get to hold their baby? Her heart cries out to hold her lost child which is no more. How empty it must be when she realizes that for this time and place it just cannot be. The emptiness that engulfs her cannot be filled. There is no one to turn to, no one who understands. The fear that she wrestles with is whether or not the child is as alone as she is. She is sorry, but her sorrow will not undo what has been done. She fears, fears that she can never be forgiven. At times she doesn't want to be forgiven. Anger rises within her, and she wishes that she could revenge herself upon those who lied to her and robbed her of her child. So, her arms are open and reaching up to God, and she dreams of the day when maybe, just maybe she will get to hold the child that she never got to hold. Oh, the sorrow that must fill millions of hearts; the emptiness that must be there every time she sees a little child playing, a baby crying, or a mother nursing. There is a poem I'd like to share with you. I am not sure who the author is, but it expresses a universal plea of all aborted women:

> If I knew then what I know now
> You never would have died
> I'd have sung you songs
> and treasured you
> more than silver more than gold
> But this song is all I'll give
> To the babe I'll never hold
>
> I've written poetry
> That hasn't been a praise;
> To the Lord who wept with me
> And held me through those days
> Jesus, now I'm asking
> I know You hear my plea,
> Won't You take the child
> in Your hands,
> And hold that babe for me?

The tragedy of abortion is seen in many ways and in many places, but I have never seen it more visibly than in the eyes of a woman who has aborted her baby, and now wants so desperately to hold it. This isn't a case of just a few women. There is a vast multitude of sad and lonely women whose only hope is that someday they will be allowed to see their baby safe in Jesus' arms. Far too many of them, those who don't know the Lord, don't even have that hope. They don't have any way of knowing His peace and forgiveness. For them their walk on earth is a lonely, living hell. That is why guilt, suicide, mourning, regret, withdrawal, hostility, anger, rage, helplessness, nightmares, seizures, frustration, alcoholism, drug abuse, and a host of other symptoms arise.

An aborted woman is suffering from a deep and abiding loss for which she blames herself and those members of society who led her down a path of self-destruction. She needs desperately to be healed by the blood of Jesus. She needs to drink of the fountain of forgiveness and everlasting life. She needs to know her sins are forgiven, especially the one that she has had such a desperate time forgiving herself for, the murder of her child. Until she comes to Christ, she will suffer, and her agony and sorrow will neither cease nor fade away.

Even if we cannot end abortion in America, we can do something to help this other victim. Against love there is no law. Even if abortion ends today, there will be the long line of living victims who will be lost and forgotten if we don't do something to give them the help they so desperately need. Every twenty seconds a baby dies. Every twenty seconds a double murder occurs. A child is dismembered and suffers a murderous death. A mother is dismembered spiritually, but her death is long and agonizing. The child is reduced to something less than the Lord intended it to be. Its mother is no better off, for from that day forward she may never be whole again. She will be left alone to suffer agonizing torture because her baby is gone and she knows deep in her heart that she killed it.

I know that the pro-abortionists are going to scream at those last words and accuse me of piling on guilt. That simply isn't so. My only intention is to help aborted women face the truth. The truth is that the pro-abortionists are not friends of women if they continue to send them to the baby butchers. They are blind guides who are sending millions of women into a living hell. They are venomous serpents who seek out women as prey and before she is able to give birth devour her child. If these same victims don't find the Lord, they are cast into a living hell for eternity. Those who prey on these women are empty tombs who walk with exalted words, but have nothing but death and decay to offer. They are hellish demons, posing as angels of light, but in truth they are in league with the angels of darkness.

If ever there was a scum of society, it is the abortionists and those who praise their treachery. Their judgment is sure, their fate set, for they will one day face the Lord of life and with Him will be all those who were their victims. These abortionists are prophets of doom, deceivers who once having milked their victim of her baby and the blood money that goes with it cast her aside with a remorseless "next."

I know that some of you are saying that we must act and deal in a loving manner even to the abortionists. I agree, we must love the abortionists and those who praise what they are doing. I love their souls, as Jesus does, but the fact is that if they continue to walk the path they are walking, they are going straight to hell. If they continue to lead souls to damnation, we must be strong to condemn their actions for what they are. That is exactly what Christ said to Peter when he stood on the side of hell: "Get behind me, Satan!" These men and women are acting as agents of Satan himself as long as they allow themselves to be used by that demonic fiend to butcher babies and ruin women and men. It's about time a number of us arise in righteous anger and call a demon a demon, and abortion what it is, murder!

That is why the Memorial must have a chapel. We need to bring suffering souls to the arms of Jesus. They have been deceived, cheated out of a precious life. Their own life has run aground upon the rocks of agony, guilt and despair. They are afraid, lonely and desperate. The only voices they are hearing are not offering them what they need, release.

Release from a terrible, terrible bondage. Sin! That's what it is. That may be an old-fashioned word, but they are bound by sin, and the sting of sin is death. Only by coming to Jesus can there be healing and release. Only by coming to Jesus can they begin to really live again. Only by coming to Jesus can they realize the depth to which they have sunk and the height to which they can climb. Oh, praise God! Praise God! For each soul that we snatch out of Satan's hands, praise God!

If you have not been released from the bonds of hell you can't begin to understand what I'm talking about. Hell on earth is a slow sure torture of the soul. It's that agonizing realization that your life is on the rocks and breaking apart. Alcohol, drugs, despair, anger, hostility, depression, guilt, suicide, nightmares, frustration, lack of drive, helplessness, and a whole host of demons invade your life. A spiritual dive is taking place that will end with your life dashed to pieces on the rocks.

It doesn't just happen overnight. It develops. At first there may be complete joy and relief. A "threat" has been eliminated and there is freedom to live your life as you want. Then, gradually, things begin to happen that cannot be explained. Feelings begin to dominate that you've never felt before, and you slowly, ever so slowly, begin to crumble inside. Often there is no way of linking what is happening to the abortion that took place so many years ago, but the link is there and it is wreaking its revenge upon your soul. Your soul knows the link and is crying out in agony and wants to die. As one woman put it: "No one ever told me I would live with this decision for the rest of my life. It's been several years now, but my grief continues."

At every Mourning Center there will be counselors. We especially need women who have been there, who know what the abortion experience can do, who have suffered loss, guilt, and anxiety, but who have been made clean through the blood of Jesus Christ. There is nothing special about these women except that they have come to know release and how it came to be. They have come to realize that Christ offered them something that others could not offer: forgiveness! With forgiveness came peace. Peace that has not been felt by some of these women for years. Peace that has not been possible until the dark, ugly sin of having killed their baby is removed. Peace that will enable them to live again, and have everlasting life. Peace that will allow them to help other women who have made the same mistake or prevent those who are about to make that mistake. Do you hear me? We need Jesus Christ in the abortion controversy because He alone has anything to offer. He alone can mend the wounds.

In reality, many women have sought other forms of assistance, but have found them inadequate and ineffective in dealing with the problems they face. A woman may share with others, and she may realize a bit of relief, but there is the bottom line of grief and anxiety that will always be there. There is the guilt that cannot be forgiven by another human being. That is God's province alone, and until she has been washed clean through the blood of Christ, there is no powerful release.

The pattern of catharsis is simple. An aborted woman knows she has sinned, and she wants to be forgiven. She needs that forgiveness from several people. She needs it from God, society, and her baby. And she needs it from herself. She also needs to forgive, for her heart is filled with anger and bitterness.

We live in a world of varied emotional experiences. For anything we do we can find a variety of reactions including both condemnation and praise. We are greatly influenced by society. If we go to the right people they will give us approval and support. They will assure us that what we have done is not serious and should be dismissed as nothing. Various elements in society are broadcasting their message of what they believe to be the truth. Some offer forgiveness, some condemnation, some praise, some criticism, and most nothing at all—they just don't care.

It is often peer pressure that influenced a woman to

have an abortion. If she had been surrounded by a different group of people, they might have influenced her to keep her baby. Another group would have opted for adoption. Intermixed would be a wide range of influence and opinions. When picketers form outside an abortion clinic they are attempting to persuade the woman who is entering to stop and keep her baby. When she gets into the clinic they are attempting to reassure her that her decision is correct and that she has every right to abort her baby. The influence doesn't end or lose its significance after the abortion is over, or the baby kept. She is daily bombarded by information that either rejects or confirms her decision. She will naturally be more receptive to information that confirms the decision that she made. If she decided to keep her baby, she will be more receptive to pro-life information. If she decided to abort her baby, she will be more receptive to pro-abortion material.

Deep within herself, however, a different process is going on. Her deep spiritual self is either confirming or rejecting her basic decision. The reason why the decision to abort has such different emotional and spiritual side-effects is that the spiritual self, deep within her, is governed by God's laws. She has violated one of the most basic of those laws, "Thou shalt not kill." Understand that this is more than a law. It is an inner spiritual principle written on our hearts. It is not like posting a 55 mile per hour speed limit. These are immutable spiritual laws that God has put in us to guide and direct our life. When we violate these spiritual laws there is inner turmoil. A woman may temporarily deal with the problem on a surface level, but her spiritual self will wrestle with it until it is able to get her to honestly deal with what she has done on a spiritual level.

What eventually happens is that deep within herself there is a decision reached that either confirms or rejects her basic decision. Her natural self has deciphered all of the information and made a decision. Her spiritual self has also made a decision. The two may not be compatible, and that is when the problems occur. Many times, and I believe the vast majority of the time, her natural decision is knowingly in contradiction to her spiritual decision.

A pastor friend of mine counseled a young girl who was a member of his congregation. She came to him to request that he baptize her baby before she took it to be aborted. The child was still in the womb and she wanted to have it baptized. She knew full well that what she was about to do was contrary to God's laws, that it was wrong. She knew full well that it was a baby, yet she felt enough outside pressure to pursue a course that eventually killed her baby. There was outside pressure from both her parents and her boyfriend to have an abortion. They were furious when the pastor attempted to talk her out of it and resigned from his congregation. It is certain that this girl will have to deal with a tremendous problem because she acted in direct violation of her own spirit which was attempting to obey God.

I am afraid that such a situation is more common than we realize. "What is legal is moral." That is the axiom so many people live by. We have got to realize that the entire human spiritual makeup contradicts that statement. We have got to realize that what the pro-abortionists have shouted all along—that you can't legislate morality—is correct. Neither can we legislate morality out of existence.

Moral, or as I prefer to call them, spiritual principles do not come from man. They come from God. God has set His standards deep within man, and they do not disappear simply because we choose not to recognize them. They are a permanent part of every person. They can be buried, but not removed. Thus, when a person chooses to violate those principles, there are deep and troubling problems that arise. The spiritual self is attuned to truth, and although a person may attempt to fool himself by acting in such a way as to deny that truth, the consequences of that action will still have their effect.

The result of denying God's law is being seen in predictable but alarming rates among women who have had an abortion. It is often difficult to make that connecting link because a whole section of society is denying that this is true. However, more and more women are starting to come forward and testify to the truth of this principle. They are doing so because they have felt its disastrous effects. Abortion is destroying America, and the pace is quickening, not because the rate of abortions is increasing, but because the number of women who have had an abortion is now excessively large.

The chapel is where an aborted woman can gain relief. Nowhere else is she offered relief in a non-threatening form. It is in the chapel that she can deal with guilt by coming to the Lord on her own behalf and on behalf of her baby. That is why we also need the signature tiles, or the "Identification Link." She must make the connection between this Memorial and her child. The signature tile is her personal connecting link to the Memorial, the child's death, and healing. When she signs the tile and places on it the information about her baby, she is linking herself to healing and hope. She has taken a big step in that direction. She is, in effect, giving her baby a resting place. She now has a grave site to go to and to mourn. She has taken a lost soul that has been in a maze and given it a place to be at peace. As she performs that simple action she senses a beginning of new peace within herself. The Memorial becomes a symbol of that peace. *It is an action that does less to* remind *her of her mistake than it does to* release *her from her mistake.* She has lived with the horror of her decision and has not been able to gain effective release from the pain of it all. Now, she can begin the journey toward her own forgiveness. That forgiveness is difficult to receive, but with proper support and understanding it can be done.

That is why there must be compassionate counselors available for her to turn to. Compassion is not enough, however; they must know how to bring her to the loving forgiveness of Jesus Christ. She will always be haunted by the reality of what she did. She will always long to hold the child that she can never hold. That emptiness cannot be breached. It can only be diminished. She will look forward to the day when she sees that child in Christ's kingdom. For now, she will learn to mourn that child's death as a mother who lost a child mourns. Someone dear and precious died, and now there is a need for healing. Her grief is legitimate. Once she has accepted that fact, she can begin to realize the healing. Once she can weep for her baby, unashamed, openly, she will begin to realize peace.

The counselors are needed to guide this whole process. They have firsthand knowledge of what she is experiencing. They are a vital link between the woman and God. They are the ones who can turn a nightmare into peace. The counselors must be born again in Jesus Christ. They have to have a call to be ministers to these women. That call is from God, and it is issued by the Holy Spirit.

If after all of this you can still say that the Memorial is nothing but mortar and concrete or that it should be built after abortion is over, you have sadly missed the message. The entire purpose of the Memorial is to bring about healing. I have not purposely neglected some other individuals involved in the need for healing—the father, grandparents, and other individuals who suffer. The Memorial and Mourning Centers are for them too. There is much work to be done to understand their grief, for it often arises out of the guilt of knowing that they pressured the woman into the abortion that they have come to see as a tragic mistake. In other cases they made a plea for the child's life, but their wife, daughter, granddaughter, or friend had no obligation to listen to that plea. There are many, many hurting fathers, grandfathers, and grandmothers who are grief-stricken because their child or grandchild was murdered by its mother and they could do nothing to stop her. They need to deal with their grief and anger. The Memorial will help them too.

It is estimated that over one million visitors will come to the Memorial each year. Many of these will be pro-life. Many others will not be sure where they stand. They will come simply because they have had an abortion and want to mourn. It would be a missed opportunity not to educate them further as to this wonderful human being, the unborn child, that is being treated as a cancerous growth inside a woman's body. With the developments that are occuring in fetology, we have come to realize how truly wonderful this life in the womb is. Every time I read some new material concerning this life, I am truly amazed at how beautiful and developed it is. We are not dealing with blobs of flesh. We are dealing with a baby who knows and is aware of much more than we ever before realized.

We have also come a long way with audiovisual presentation and animation. It will be the purpose of the Memorial to present this life as accurately and dramatically as technologically possible. We need the casual observer to be struck by the awesomeness of this tiny life. To do that we will employ the best available people to develop the most effective ways of presenting our tiny friends. They deserve a fair hearing, and certainly the atmosphere of the Memorial and the opportunity it presents must not be neglected. Thus, there will be both an auditorium and an education center. There will be numerous teaching devices, including examples of devices now used to end that life. Once people come to realize the damage that abortion is doing to both mother and child, they will realize the degree to which injustice prevails in this society.

Surrounding all of this will be roses. Roses of all kinds, sizes, and colors. Roses are a fitting symbol of the child in the womb. The beauty of the rose will do much to enhance the concept that the child in the womb is beautiful and delicate too. Like the rose, the child needs to be nurtured and loved for it to blossom into the beautiful life that God intended it to be.

The time to build the Memorial and the Mourning Centers is now. They are needed immediately, to help the current victims and to put an end to abortion for good. We need dedicated people who will support them with their prayers, actions, and financial resources.

ELEVEN

The Key
Ingredient

Though I speak with the tongues of men and of angels, and have not love, I am become as a sounding brass, or a clanging cymbal . . . *1 Corinthians 13:1*

There are many words spoken about the need for love and the results that it produces. I am not going to elaborate on them, but there is something that needs to be said, and it has to do with love.

And though I bestow all my goods to feed the poor, and though I give my body to be burned, and have not love, it profits me nothing. *1 Corinthians 13:3*

Recently a television reporter referred to me on a news broadcast saying, "This man really hates abortion." Although what he had ascertained after interviewing me at length was broadcast in the negative, what he had experienced was not just a hatred for abortion but a love for children. To love what is just and true requires that we abhor and hate that which is not. On another occasion I was asked what drives me so hard to end abortion. Why am I so involved? After the person had asked me that, he seemed to shrink back fearing that he had trampled upon holy or sacred ground. My reply was both honest and simple. God has placed upon my heart a deep love for the unborn. I truly weep when I realize that each day another four thousand plus babies die in the United States. How many die each day across the world? I have heard various figures and they make me sick inside. Our world is suffering from a serious lack of love—love that will sacrifice for someone, love that calls for us to care enough to become involved, love that doesn't dispose of babies as if they were trash. That is the kind of love that is sadly absent from the world and is needed ever so badly.

Love is the key. The sad truth is that too few individuals are deeply, lovingly committed to the unborn child and the mother who carries that child. That is part of the reason so little to stop abortion has been accomplished to date. Without love, we cannot hope to conquer the enemy. This is the enemy that rips babies apart and charges for the privilege. This is the enemy that has rocked millions and millions of people to sleep in a stupor of apathy. When will we begin to awaken? When will we begin to love?

Those who have the strongest, deepest, gentlest love are the women who have come through the abortion experience and found healing in Jesus Christ. They understand what love is, for it abides deep within their soul. They have what is too evidently missing from far too many who make up the pro-life camp. They will not be fooled or lied to anymore. They love the unborn child and its struggling mother, and they aren't afraid to be vocal about it. Their love is committed.

That is one of the primary reasons I see the future of the pro-life camp vested in those women who have had an abortion and have come to the loving forgiveness of Christ. Women like those of WEBA have that love, and it is that love that drives them forward. It is the element of that love that gives them strength in the face of suffering, criticism, loneliness, and sorrow. They know what they are fighting for and why. They have been released from an ocean of sorrow, and they don't want someone else to go through what they have. They don't want someone else's baby to die. They really love one another.

They express their love for one another in a very open

way. If you ever attend an open WEBA meeting you will see a lot of hugging and tears. They hug, they hold, they cry, they laugh, they truly love. Theirs is a kinship of tears and victory in Jesus Christ. When they talk about their life and the mistake they made, there is both determination and sorrow. They have known the pits of blackness and now are being led to the mountaintop of hope. You can see the love they have for one another radiating from their heart. Jesus said that the one who is forgiven much, loves much. They love very much indeed.

There is no way to instill that love within someone. You either have it or you don't. For me, there was no deep, mysterious happening in my past that put a burning love for the unborn on my heart. The Lord put it there, and I am grateful that He did. For them, the WEBA women, there is the ugly past that they have secretly wrestled with for years, and from which they had tried desperately to escape. They had believed lies, been pressured, and ultimately robbed of something very precious. With the loss of their baby went the loss of dignity. With the loss of dignity went the loss of their life. For many of them there was no one to turn to. They had either all left, didn't want to hear, or couldn't understand. The struggle of a woman who has had an abortion is a very lonely one. There is no pity, nor does she want any, but she does need love and understanding. She needs someone to understand that she misses her baby. She needs someone to understand that she is frightened and feels terrible. It is no wonder that many commit suicide or turn to escape mechanisms such as drugs. The world doesn't care, doesn't love.

"So she had an abortion, so what?"

"It was her choice. She knew what she was doing."

"Don't come to me and cry. You made your choice, now live with it."

The list of excuses goes on and on, but the bottom line is, "Who cares! Just don't bother me with your weeping." The sum total of it all is that she is alone, and no one seems to care.

In the Gospel of Luke (7:36-50) we have an interesting story about Jesus when He was at the house of Peter. A woman who was a sinner enters. It goes like this:

> Now one of the Pharisees was requesting Him to dine with him. And He entered the Pharisee's house, and reclined at the table. And behold, there was a woman in the city who was a sinner; and when she learned that He was reclining at the table in the Pharisee's house, she brought an alabaster vial of perfume, and standing behind Him at His feet, weeping, she began to wet His feet with her tears, and kept wiping them with the hair of her head, and kissing His feet, and anointing them with the perfume. Now when the Pharisee who had invited Him saw this he said to himself, "If this man were a prophet He would know who and what sort of person this woman is who is touching Him, that she is a sinner." And Jesus answered and said to him, "Simon, I have something to say to you." And he replied, "Say it, teacher."
>
> "A certain moneylender had two debtors: one owed five hundred denarii, and the other fifty. When they were unable to repay, he graciously forgave them both. Which of them therefore will love him more?"
>
> Simon answered and said, "I suppose the one whom he forgave more." And He said to him, "You have judged correctly." And turning to the woman he said to Simon, "Do you see this woman? I entered your house; you gave Me no water for My feet, but she has wet My feet with her tears, and wiped them with her hair. You gave Me no kiss; but she, since the time I came in has not ceased to kiss My feet. You did not anoint My head with oil, but she anointed My feet with perfume. For this reason I say to you, her sins, which are many have been forgiven, for she loved much; but he who is forgiven little, loves little." And He said to her, "Your sins have been forgiven." And those who were reclining at the table with Him began to say to themselves, "Who is this man who

even forgives sins?" And He said to the woman, "Your faith has saved you; go in peace."

To understand deep love you have to have an understanding of deep sorrow. To understand the love that these women have for the Lord is impossible unless you have been where they have. That is not a thing to be desired. If their love for the Lord and for the lives that have been destroyed is any indication, they have been forgiven much, very, very much. They have something which the other side can never understand, for if they did, they would not be on the other side. They would cease criticism of those who have come out of that hell and rejoice with them.

There is no way to fill the individuals who have not come through the fire with the same love. What we can do is fill the pro-life movement with those who have. We need the Mourning Centers and the National Memorial to reach out to the most powerful force we can muster, the power of those whose sin has been forgiven, who have been set free by Jesus Christ. They will bring that key ingredient to this struggle, the ingredient that up till now has been largely missing. They will bring love, and love never fails.

TWELVE

What Now?

The Pro-Life Manifesto will do no good if it does not arouse action. Action must never be left to someone else, for if it is it will surely never get done. If you read this manifesto and say, "That's a great idea, I hope it works!" and do nothing to help make it a reality, you have missed the point. You will have done the pro-life cause a great disservice. To do nothing is to act on behalf of the abortionists! That is exactly what they want you to do!

This is a "How To" chapter. The cause is in need of people who will step forward and get things done. We don't need any more cheerleaders on the sidelines. We need players in the thick of the action. This is not a spectator event; you are part of a life or death situation. If you are still uncertain of what we are about and why, read this book again. You must understand the strategy if you are to be effective. Once you understand the strategy, you will know how to get involved. Then, all you will need to do is get involved. If you wonder if it's all worth it, count to 1,500,000 and multiply it times the number of years that have passed since 1973! Impossible? No, for it was by single human lives that we have reached that figure of actual lives lost. No big masses of deaths—just one here and one there, but each one counting. You count too! Make a difference.

To accomplish the objectives of the Pro-Life Manifesto, which will destroy abortion from within, we must accomplish the following things:

1) We must build the National Memorial to the Unborn Child, *and we must do it now!*
2) We must establish regional Mourning Centers, *and we must do it immediately!*
3) We need to build up the organization called WEBA, Women Exploited By Abortion. *They are our dynamite!*
4) We need to form chapters of Heart Light across the United States to assist in all of the above. *Start one today!*
5) We need to urge other pro-life groups to understand and support the objectives of the Pro-Life Manifesto. *We must have unity!*
6) We have to end all of the unproductive efforts and concentrate our energy toward the above five goals. *Otherwise, we will be defeated!*

THE NATIONAL MEMORIAL TO THE UNBORN CHILD

There are several things that you can do to help make the Memorial a reality:

1) Make a donation to the Memorial.

Check payable to:
HEART LIGHT MEMORIAL
Box 8513
Green Bay, WI 54308
(All donations are tax-deductible)

2) A donation of $100 or more will entitle you to have your name on the Pool of Tears. With your donation please indicate: POOL OF TEARS. Print your name, address, and phone number very carefully. Husbands and wives may donate together and will both be placed on. We have a limited amount of space, and that is on a first come, first served basis.

3) Send for brochures about the Memorial. They are free. Distribute them to as many people as possible. Better yet, buy enough copies of this book for your friends!

4) Help raise funds for the Memorial. Have a "Quarters for Life" drive. Every quarter raised will represent one life. If we collect one quarter for each child killed in abortion since 1973, we can build the Memorial! Collect quarters!

5) Understand fully what the Memorial can accomplish! This is critical.

THE REGIONAL MOURNING CENTERS

For the Mourning Centers to be effective, they must include the following factors: a WEBA chapter, a Planning Committee, and funding. They are to be built across the country in all major population areas.

1) Form a Heart Light chapter in your community if there isn't one already. (See the section in this chapter about that.)

2) Make a donation to the Mourning Center project. Specify which one. If you aren't sure if there is one in your area, just specify your area. There will be one started soon, and you may be providing the seed to do it. If you wish, it can go to an existing project that needs help.

3) Determine if there is a WEBA chapter in your area. If there is, contact them about your desire to build a Mourning Center in your area, and see what you can do to help. You will be welcomed with open arms!

4) Spread the word about the Mourning Center concept, and send for free brochures for distribution.

5) Sponsor me, or a representative of the Memorial-Mourning Center project, to come and address your group. The only cost is expenses, and we try to live on pennies.

6) Write Heart Light for a *Mourning Center Study Guide* (cost: $25). It will explain in detail all you will need to know to get a Mourning Center going where you are. This could be an important step for your community.

WEBA: WOMEN EXPLOITED BY ABORTION

1) Make a donation to your local WEBA chapter and/ or to National WEBA.

Send and make the check to:
WEBA
202 S. Andrews
Three Rivers, MI 49093
(616) 273-8476

WEBA National can tell you who is in your area and how to get in contact with them. Lorijo Nerad, the president, is a wonderful individual who will do all she can to assist you.

2) Invite a WEBA speaker to your group's next meeting. It will leave you more aware of how powerful this group is.

3) Support the National Memorial to the Unborn Child and the Mourning Centers. They are designed to help WEBA become a powerful force in the pro-life movement. By helping them you are helping other women be set free from bondage.

4) Learn more about women who have had an abortion and the problems they face. It will help you understand that there is a second victim of abortion, and a sadly neglected one at that.

HEART LIGHT CHAPTERS

Heart Light chapters are local pro-life groups that are formed to carry out the objectives of the Pro-Life Manifesto. For an existing pro-life group, you can become "A Friend of Heart Light" and support the efforts being made.

1) Write to Heart Light and request more information about forming a chapter.

2) Talk to your pro-life group about the importance of the objectives of the manifesto.

PROMOTING THE OBJECTIVES OF THE MANIFESTO

If you are convinced that the Pro-Life Manifesto is on the right track, then please promote it. You can do so in a number of ways.

1) Recommend the book to others.
2) Send for copies of the book and distribute them among your friends or group. There are special rates available for quantities.
3) Contact your local Christian bookstore and request that they carry an adequate supply of books. If they don't have it, request that they stock it.

HELP OTHER GROUPS AND INDIVIDUALS UNDERSTAND THE PRINCIPLES INVOLVED

There is much that you can do. These items are intended to show you what some of them are. It takes courage to be a pioneer, but there are plenty of rewards as well. The battle for life does not have the luxury of time, since every twenty seconds another child loses its life.

We really do need to hear from you. The children facing death need you to care. Please act generously and effectively. We can win this war, but it will take more than talk. It will take a careful, effective strategy that will not fail. We have it, now let's use it!

Our address is as follows:

HEART LIGHT
Box 8513
Green Bay, WI 54308
(414) 468-8444

God bless you! May you and I join as partners to end this deadly plague in our land. Let's put an end to the number one killer of babies and the number one destroyer of lives—abortion. May our Lord Jesus Christ give us the power to do just that.

One last word. I mean it when I say that I *need* and *want* to hear from you. Without you things won't work. *You* are important! Make the difference. Let me close with a quote that I ended Chapter 1 with:

> Rescue those who are unjustly sentenced to death; don't stand back and let them die. Don't try to disclaim responsibility by saying you didn't know about it. For God, who knows all hearts, knows yours, and He knows that you knew! And He will reward everyone according to his deeds (Proverbs 24:11-12).